HOW TO MAKE MONEY IN *ANY* REAL ESTATE MARKET

HOW TO MAKE MONEY IN *ANY* REAL ESTATE MARKET

ROBERT E. LAWLESS

Westport, Connecticut
London

Library of Congress Cataloging-in-Publication Data

Lawless, Robert E., 1966–
    How to make money in any real estate market / Robert E. Lawless.
        p. cm.
    Includes bibliographical references and index.
    ISBN 978–0–313–36550–8 (alk. paper)
1. Real estate investment—United States. 2. Real estate investment. I. Title.
HD255.L37   2009
332.63'240973—dc22   2008051403

British Library Cataloguing in Publication Data is available.

Library of Congress Catalog Card Number: 2008051403
ISBN: 978–0–313–36550–8

First published in 2009

Praeger Publishers, 88 Post Road West, Westport, CT 06881
An imprint of Greenwood Publishing Group, Inc.
www.praeger.com

Printed in the United States of America

The paper used in this book complies with the
Permanent Paper Standard issued by the National
Information Standards Organization (Z39.48–1984).

10 9 8 7 6 5 4 3 2 1

CONTENTS

FOREWORD

Obviously you, the reader, have the right mind-set toward real estate investing or you would not be reading *How to Make Money in* Any *Real Estate Market.* Too many people buy and sell real estate at inopportune times and unfavorable prices and terms based upon intuition, unrealistic investment strategies, and poor advice. Robert Lawless to the rescue! Whether you are a seasoned real estate veteran or an investment neophyte full of curious wonder, this book will provide sage advice and will serve as your main real estate market reference guide for years to come.

After thirty-plus years in the real estate industry as an investor, operator, and business owner, I still subscribe to the adage, "If you stand in the same place too long, you will get run over by your market." As is often the case with any investment opportunity, prudent and timely action dictates success or failure. Understanding how to make money in any real estate market will allow you to avoid costly mistakes due to inaction or misguided action. Robert lays out a plethora of real estate principles that will allow you to create quantitative and qualitative real estate investment strategies that will succeed no matter the real estate environment.

As you will see, Robert is able to articulate sound real estate principles masterfully and communicate clearly lessons learned over decades of real estate investment experience in various sectors of both the real estate and the lending industries. These are the same general principles that well-known, successful real estate investors utilize and rely upon on a daily basis.

As I sit here today watching another triple-digit stock market decline and reading more of the negative press condemning the real estate industry, it is easy to stand still or panic based upon the doom-and-gloom outlook flowing from the media. But mass fear creates great investment opportunities for the savvy and well-trained investor. Do not get caught standing still too long. Enjoy reading this book, creating or recreating money making strategies, and taking advantage of the enormous real estate investment opportunities in this market cycle and the many market cycles to come.

Tom Banks
President, Greenfield Real Estate Companies
Former Regional Vice President, Lennar Homes Corporation

ACKNOWLEDGMENTS

I would like to thank my wife, Tanya, for her continued support of my various career endeavors. She has been a great inspiration and has allowed me the time to write and pursue other interests by skillfully managing the many complexities associated with the lives of our family. In addition, she has been overly tolerant, outgoing, and supportive of our many moves around the country and abroad. I continue to enjoy the experiences and diversity that we encounter through our travels and each day seems to present new opportunities and adventures. For her nonstop efforts and years of support, encouragement, and contribution, I dedicate this book to her.

INTRODUCTION

While there are great fortunes to be made through real estate investing, there are also great fortunes to be lost. In many cases, there is a winner (someone who makes money) and a loser (someone who loses money). This is usually the case in down markets when an individual, or an entity, owned real estate that experienced a significant reduction in value. The seller sold at a loss and a buyer with longer term insight or greater financial strength saw an opportunity.

Under other circumstances, there are only winners. In such cases, each owner of a particular piece of property makes money before selling to the next owner. For example, a vacant piece of land may go through numerous stages of development and many owners before ultimately being used to build a residential community or commercial structure. As the land becomes more and more developed, it increases in value. Later, the ultimate owners of the completed houses or commercial buildings may continue to sell for additional profits. Such happy scenarios are usually the result of steady and rising markets.

Sometimes, a specific property neither goes up in value nor declines in value for extended periods of time. Such flat market conditions are clearly better for property owners than markets that are deteriorating. But unless there is some expected appreciation in the future, property owners under this scenario are often actually losing money due to inflationary pressures and the fact that a dollar in the future should be worth more than a dollar today.

Each of these general market conditions presents challenges and opportunities for prudent investors who have thought ahead and planned for the expected and the unexpected. Real estate cycles can last for years and even decades. In addition, direct real estate ownership often results in illiquidity, meaning that buying and selling property usually takes a substantial amount of time and can include large transaction costs. Selling too quickly might require significant price concessions. Buying too hastily may result in overpayment and unforeseen problems.

The purpose of this book is to identify and clearly communicate the lessons that I have learned after working and investing within the real estate and lending industries for over two decades. I have seen many people earn incredible sums of money in short periods of time. I have also seen real estate investors and developers lose anywhere from a few thousand dollars to many tens of millions of dollars on a single transaction. Some of these losses could have been avoided with differing mentalities, financing structures, and investment strategies. Others were bound to fail from the start.

Some real estate investors are lacking in financial expertise. Others are poor planners that base their investments on illogical or nonexistent strategies and projections. Another category of investors includes those without enough creativity or flexibility—or maybe they just give up too easily. Some investors get lucky and ride favorable market conditions. Others bet the farm and lose.

No one can time the real estate markets perfectly, and virtually anyone can make money in a rapidly rising market just through dumb luck. But the better real estate investors will generally know when to buy and when to sell. They will be able to maintain control over their properties under adverse circumstances. They will know how to work with lenders and how to find and evaluate the highest and best uses for a particular piece of property. These are the people that can make money in any real estate market.

There are certainly many horror stories about real estate investing. These outcomes are most common during down real estate markets. When real estate markets turn ugly, these cycles can last for many years. And when you are dealing with a leveraged, high-dollar-cost, and illiquid asset that cannot be sold quickly without a large price reduction, it is pretty easy to see how financial devastation can result.

When the guy that bought a series of single-family homes expecting to flip them in a few months for huge profits is stuck with no tenants and multiple mortgage payments, it does not take long before the banks start to foreclose. When a real estate developer's project takes longer than expected and he only raised enough capital to cover a predetermined period of time, his options can become limited. When a local or regional economy turns downward, there can be many adverse repercussions. Companies may begin laying off employees and downsizing their operations, which will ultimately result in lower demand for housing and higher vacancies for commercial space. The owners of these properties need to have adequate capital to continue paying property financing and maintenance costs.

At the time of this writing in late 2008, the residential housing market in the United States is in a dismal state. Under such conditions, it is easy to see the downsides to real estate investing, because so many people are feeling the mental and financial pain associated with owning properties that are unsalable and rapidly dropping in value. The supply of homes vastly exceeds the supply of willing buyers and a bottom has yet to be found. Large publicly traded home builders are writing off hundreds of millions of dollars in land costs. The daily press is more depressing each day as more homes continue to come on the market due to borrower defaults and foreclosures. In fact, the problems seem so severe that the federal government continues to work with lending institutions and seeks other means to prop up the economy and protect homeowners.

While billions of dollars will be lost by real estate investors of varying size, form, and level of sophistication during this cycle, another group of investors will seize the countless current and upcoming opportunities. In fact, billions of dollars of capital has been set aside by many individuals and entities in order to capitalize on the misfortunes of others. Many of these investors made substantial sums of money before the residential housing cycle peaked and they will continue to make money because of its declines. My intent is to convey many of the primary strategies used by the people behind these investment decisions within this writing.

If you have read my first book, *Retire Richer and Faster! You Can Manage Your Own Financial Independence!*, you know that real estate is one of my favorite investment choices. This is why the majority of my professional career has centered on various forms of real estate lending and investing. While one specific chapter was devoted to real estate within my prior book, many of the principles described in other chapters also pertain to real estate investing. But there is so much more to cover and so many benefits associated with this topic that I felt the need to write an entire book on the subject.

I welcome you to join me on the journey to becoming a better real estate investor. As stated earlier, anyone can make money in the right real estate market simply investing by chance. However, making money in all real estate markets requires a specific skill set. Once acquired, this knowledge truly defines, differentiates, and elevates a person from the many people who call themselves real estate investors, yet lack the information and sustainable investment strategies needed to succeed in all markets.

Chapter 1

WHY I LIKE REAL ESTATE

There are many reasons why real estate remains my favorite investment alternative. While I am a firm believer in diversifying my total portfolio among various investments such as domestic and foreign stocks and bonds, cash, and other asset classes, real estate has always played a significant role.

Lenders are often more compelled to provide loans backed by real estate because real estate is a tangible asset that tends to hold its value. Real estate ownership can provide favorable tax benefits through deductions for such items as interest expense and depreciation. In addition, sometimes real estate projects can receive tax credits and other favorable treatment from local and federal governments when beneficial to a community.

Real estate can also be a great investment to protect against the risks associated with inflation. In addition, real estate has proven itself to generate strong historic investment returns. We will talk more about each of these benefits below and throughout the book.

THE ABILITY TO BORROW

As will be further discussed in Chapter 4, "The Benefits and Risks of Leverage," lenders are often more willing to lend when real estate is the underlying collateral for their loans. Investors can borrow against qualifying stocks and bonds, but often only up to 50% of their values as limited by law (depending on the lender). In addition, usually the borrowing rates do not become attractive until you are willing and able to borrow very large amounts of money (over $500,000). There is also the potential risk for margin calls. A lender will require you to put up more cash each time your investment values decline below a certain threshold. I do not like this uncertainty or the fact that the stocks and bonds supporting such borrowings are constantly trading in the capital markets and their prices move up and down all the time (i.e., there is price volatility).

Investors can often borrow against non–real estate assets or even on an unsecured basis. But normally such borrowings are for fairly short periods of time. In addition, loans may have financial conditions and restrictions that must be maintained and the interest rates are usually higher than when borrowing against tangible and more generic assets like real estate.

When you borrow against real estate, you are not subject to margin calls and, besides making your payments each month, you generally do not have to communicate with your lender once the loan has closed. Even if your property value declines, many types of loans never require any type of prepayment as long as you make your scheduled payments. In addition, most real estate loans are so standardized that they have minimal closing costs and you can borrow for long periods of time at attractive interest rates.

THE MATH WORKS

There are many favorable economic benefits to owning real estate. For example, buildings and other physical structures are depreciated for tax purposes. Depreciation is a noncash expense that is beneficial to real estate investors due to the tax deductions that it provides. The general idea behind depreciation is that residential and commercial buildings, improvements, and fixtures tend to lose their values over time as a result of wear and tear, age, and obsolescence.

Depending on the depreciation method used, the value of a building might be depreciated for tax purposes over a period of 20 to 30 years. For example, assume you purchase a commercial building for $500,000. Also assume that when you bought the property an appraisal showed a value of $200,000 for the underlying land and $300,000 for the building. This means that you will be depreciating the $300,000 building each year until its value for tax purposes is reduced to zero.

Land is not depreciated because it is assumed to hold its value. But buildings are depreciated because the accountants believe that their values will decline over time and that they will ultimately become worthless. Such misconceptions prove highly beneficial for real estate owners. We all know that even when a building is 30 years old, it is still a valuable piece of property (assuming that it has been properly maintained). In fact, during the past 30 years, the property probably increased in value many times over. Tenants still want to rent older properties and buyers still want to purchase older properties.

So while investors are deducting depreciation expense on their annual tax returns, which assumes the value of a property is steadily declining, usually the opposite is taking place. Real estate generally tends to increase in value over time. Therefore, investors are receiving tax deductions and lower tax bills each year, while their investment values are actually increasing! This is a gift provided to real estate investors by the federal government.

Interest expense is another cost item that can significantly reduce an investor's tax obligation. Just like maintenance and repair costs are deductions that lower the amount of income that a property is generating, so is the interest expense associated with financing the purchase and ownership of a property.

As you will see in the chapter on leverage, buying property using someone else's money, such as a bank or other type of lender, can greatly enhance investor profitability. In addition, borrowing most of the money needed to buy a property allows investors to substantially increase their purchasing power and buy more and larger properties.

To better illustrate how the tax benefits from depreciation and interest expense are derived, let us look at the following example in Table 1.1.

Table 1.1 shows the benefits that depreciation and interest expense deductions can provide when looking at a hypothetical investor's tax obligations under two scenarios. Both scenarios show a rental property that generates $45,000 of annual rental income. Without expense items to offset this income, the property owner would be forced to pay income taxes on the entire $45,000. However, normal property expenses such as maintenance and repair costs and property management fees are allowable tax deductions when computing income tax obligations.

Scenario 1 shows the interest expense and depreciation associated with the property. When these expenses are included with the other property-related costs, the property generates an annual net loss of $4,450 for tax purposes. Because of this loss, the investor does not have any tax obligation associated with the property. In fact, he has a tax credit that may be used to offset other taxable income. Assuming the investor can use this tax credit, the government now owes the investor $1,113 because of the loss produced from his property.

Scenario 2 looks at the same property but shows what happens when interest expense and depreciation are not included. Because these items provide such large tax deductions, their removal results in net property income of $34,550 and the investor is forced to pay the government $8,638 in taxes for the year. As you can see, interest expense and depreciation result in huge tax benefits for real estate investors.

Table 1.1
Tax Benefits of Interest Expense and Depreciation

	Scenario 1	Scenario 2
Rental income	$ 45,000	$ 45,000
Maintenance costs	(2,250)	(2,250)
Repair costs	(5,000)	(5,000)
Property management	(2,700)	(2,700)
Professional fees	(500)	(500)
Interest expense	(24,000)	–
Depreciation	(15,000)	–
Net property income/(loss)	$ (4,450)	$ 34,550
Taxes due/(tax credit)	$ (1,113)	$ 8,638
(assumes 25% tax rate)		

TAX CREDITS

Federal and local governments sometimes provide incentives to motivate real estate investors to develop and improve certain buildings, sites, and communities. For example, the federal government allows tax credits to be taken by investors when restoring buildings placed in service before 1936 and for certified historic structures. Generally, a percentage of the costs invested into a designated structure will qualify as a tax credit. For example, for every $100 in costs, a real estate investor may receive $20 in tax credits that can be used to subsidize project costs and to offset other taxable income.

Tax credits may also be awarded for improvements to low-income areas as well. Low-income housing tax credits are awarded to real estate developers and investors by each state in an effort to provide inexpensive housing to low-income families. Tax credits are also being provided by the federal government for commercial real estate projects in an effort to create jobs, improve streets, and revitalize specific areas and communities.

Tax credits and additional tax deductions are sometimes available for other real estate initiatives such as for the construction of energy-efficient homes and buildings and the installation of solar power. Rules pertaining to such tax credits and deductions can change and vary depending on particular locations and local governments. When applicable, how such potential tax benefits pertain to your specific investment and situation should be discussed with your tax advisor. For now, just realize that when available, such tax credits and deductions can greatly enhance the profitability of real estate investments.

INFLATION PROTECTION

Inflation can be defined as a rise in the general prices of goods and services within a particular country. These goods and services include the costs for housing, automobiles, and groceries. The cost of a gallon of milk is now about $4. You can bet that milk did not cost nearly this much 20 years ago. Nor did an average car cost $20,000. The gradual increase of prices over time has been caused by inflation.

Inflation can reduce the value of an investment and adversely affect investor profitability. For example, if your investment is earning 3% per year and the annual inflation rate for the country is 4%, you are effectively losing 1% per year on your investment. This is because your money is growing at a lesser rate than the increase in prices for the goods and services that it can buy.

Real estate has a fairly strong correlation with inflation. As the prices for goods and services rise within an economy, rents and property values generally increase as well. In periods of high inflation, real estate values have tended to rise faster than in periods of lower inflation. In addition, lease rates on real estate can usually be increased based upon the level of inflation. If you are renting a single-family home to a tenant under a one-year lease, chances are that you can raise the rent by a larger amount at the end of the lease in periods of high inflation versus periods of low inflation. Hence, investors often view their real estate investments as insurance or a "hedge" against inflation.

Many long-term property leases have rental rates tied to an annual rate of inflation. For example, a particular lease may have contractual terms that require the tenant to pay annual increases based upon a country's prior year's rate of inflation. The longer a lease on a property, the greater the need to have some type of escalation clause so that the rent a tenant pays continues to rise over time.

Assume a grocery store is leasing its store space from a property owner at a rate of 8% for the first year of its lease. Also assume that the lease terms require the grocer to pay an increase in annual rent in the second year based upon the prior year's inflation rate. If the inflation rate was 3% in the prior year, then the second year lease rate would increase to 8.24% (8% times 1.03). By using such an escalation clause, the owner of the property has protected his investment against the risks of inflation.

INVESTMENT PERFORMANCE

Real estate has historically shown impressive investment profitability and has provided excellent diversification benefits when included within a larger portfolio of investments. Since most individual property purchases and sales are negotiated and executed on a private basis, there are no public markets where buyers and sellers transact. In addition, there are few compilations that broadly show how various types of real estate investments have performed over time. However, we can look at the profitability of publicly traded companies that specifically invest in real estate for an indication of real estate's historic performance.

Real estate investment trusts, or "REITs," will be discussed more in later chapters. For now, just know that REITs were created to passively own and invest in multiple types of real estate, including hotels, warehouses, office buildings, and retail shopping centers. The National Association of Real Estate Investment Trusts, or "NAREIT," is an association that tracks the performance of publicly traded REITs.

As indicated in Chart 1.1, we can see how the NAREIT Equity REIT Index has historically performed when compared to the S&P 500 Index, which tracks the stocks of the 500 largest U.S. companies and is considered a benchmark for the performance of the overall U.S. stock market.

Chart 1.1
Historical Investment Performance

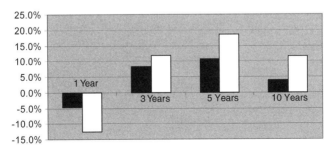

Chart 1.1 shows the average annual returns provided to investors for varying periods of time as of April 30, 2008. We can see that REITs have performed significantly better than the S&P 500 Index for the past three-, five-, and ten-year periods. While the REIT Index has underperformed the S&P 500 Index for the past one-year period, most investment returns are more meaningful when considered on a longer term basis.

Real estate can be a great source of diversification when part of a larger portfolio consisting of multiple asset classes such as domestic and foreign stocks, bonds and other investments. Portfolio diversification can often lead to lower risk and higher investor profitability when compared to nondiversified portfolios. In addition, diversification tends to smooth investment volatility resulting in greater overall portfolio stability.

SUMMARY

Real estate has proven itself to be a great investment vehicle. As mentioned above, there are numerous benefits associated with real estate investing. Real estate serves as excellent borrowing collateral and real estate loans often have low interest rates and closing costs. The federal government provides tax benefits through the deductibility of interest expense, depreciation, and other costs and by providing specific tax credits and deductions to support community development and improvement. Real estate can also provide protection against the adverse effects that inflation can have on many investments. Lastly, real estate has provided impressive historic investment returns and serves as an excellent source of portfolio diversification.

Chapter 2

WHAT DRIVES REAL ESTATE VALUES?

There are many types of properties. Some of the key sectors that serve as real estate investments include single-family houses and condominiums, multifamily homes and apartments, agricultural, industrial/manufacturing, warehouse storage and distribution, office, hospitality (i.e., hotels and resorts), retail, mixed use (like a property with both retail shopping and condominiums), and special purpose (like an arena, golf course, or marina). Each sector provides its own risks and potential rewards.

There are many general drivers of real estate value. Some of these are more unique to a specific sector, but many are applicable across all or most sectors. Many will find the discussion regarding the topics below unsurprising and plain commonsense, but many real estate investors nevertheless tend to overlook some of these concepts.

WHAT CAN I DO WITH THIS PROPERTY?

The underlying value of real estate can be tied not only to its current use but also to its potential future use. Just because a property is being used as an apartment building today does not mean that the property value cannot be substantially increased by converting the apartments into condominium units. A dilapidated house may not appear to have much value, but the underlying land may be in a desirable location. Perhaps someone would buy the property, remove the existing house, and build another. Land being used for farming today might be worth much more if used for residential housing or a retail shopping center. It takes a visionary to see a path and follow it.

Just because a real estate investor wants to use a certain piece of property for a specific use does not mean that this is always possible. Cities and municipalities dictate the available uses for a piece of property through their zoning laws. You would not want an industrial factory that produces toxic waste and foul smells directly next door to a retail shopping center. Nor would you want a baseball arena next to a residential housing community. Zoning laws are used to protect citizens and to better shape a region's development patterns, but they can also present challenges for real estate investors.

Some real estate investors are better equipped to deal with political zoning officials than others. Existing and favorable relationships, good reputations, and strong communication and presentation skills are attributes that can aid in obtaining a favorable zoning decision. Investors also need to think about how their projects are going to benefit a specific city or region and effectively articulate these points to the right people.

Other factors that can substantially increase a property's value include such benefits as access to water, roads, and rail. An inaccessible property's value might increase many fold after the decision to construct an adjacent major highway is announced. A property having no rights to water will have limited use. Acquiring such rights can materially increase its value.

Factors that can reduce a property's value include environmental and flooding problems. Buying a piece of property that was once a gas station may lead to huge environmental cleanup costs before another type of business can be opened. A property prone to flooding will either need to be fixed or its value will be heavily discounted.

We will talk more about finding a property's highest and best uses throughout the book. For now, just realize that a key value driver for investment real estate is based upon a property's current and potential uses and the rights that go with it.

SIMPLE ECONOMICS

At some time or another, most of us have heard the reference to the economic forces of supply and demand. Supply and demand is the underlying concept between the free exchange of capital and goods and services within a country and often among countries. If something is in high demand and in limited supply, the price will normally increase until a better balance exists. For example, perhaps 100 consumers are willing to buy a computer for $1,000. At $1,500, there may only be 60 buyers. At $500, there may be 2,000 buyers. If a seller of computers has only 50 in stock, she might raise the price to $1,500 in order to maximize profits.

The same concept applies to real estate. Demand in excess of supply will generally drive prices upward. Supply in excess of demand will normally drive prices downward. The demand for a particular property may be driven by various factors, including its current quality or future use potential, zoning changes, and expected growth in the general geographic area. Whatever the reason for the demand, the point is that the more people wanting a property, the greater the chance that it can be sold at a higher price. Inversely, when you have few or no interested buyers, your pricing power and your ability to sell a property becomes much more limited.

Using a recent example, consider the run-up in housing prices that occurred from around 2000 through 2007. There was very strong demand from buyers seeking new residences, but also from speculative real estate investors. These investors were betting that housing prices would continue to rise and that properties could be quickly sold at a profit. This level of demand continued to push prices higher and higher until the prices were so high that there were no longer enough buyers to support the inventory of homes on the market. At this point, supply began to exceed demand and prices started to fall. Factors that continue to add houses to the market include bank foreclosures, investors attempting to sell properties, and more home buyers sitting on the sidelines awaiting lower prices. How far prices will fall before a closer equilibrium between supply and demand is achieved has yet to be seen.

DEMOGRAPHICS

The demographics of a particular region can play a significant role regarding the value of real estate. The demographics of a specific population define the types of people living in a certain area by grouping by categories such as age, income, occupation, and education.

When evaluating real estate, the current and projected demographics of a specific region can be a very important consideration. A key factor that serves to support real estate values is a stable and increasing population size. The more people living in a certain area, the greater the need for residential housing. In addition, the more occupied homes in an area, the greater the need for commercial real estate to support businesses that target labor pools and provide services for these people.

There are certain aspects of a particular state or region that can attract or repel people. Examples include income tax structures, weather conditions, the supply of jobs, housing costs and overall affordability, commuting time, and sources of entertainment.

The supply of jobs is a strong motivator for people to move to or remain within and around a certain city. Businesses consider numerous variables when deciding where to locate offices, factories, stores, and other activities. They do not want unfavorable tax treatment from local governments, but they do want a strong supply of available and affordable labor. Moving a distribution center to the desert may provide very inexpensive rent, but if workers are unwilling to commute to such a place, this would not be a wise decision. Building a factory dependent upon blue-collar workers in the middle of Beverly Hills would also be a poor choice.

When looking at a particular piece of property, consider the surrounding demographics, but also the current and expected demographic trends. For example, are more people moving to a certain area or leaving? Such considerations can be relevant to a particular section of town or broader to include entire states and regions. If a major improvement initiative is underway or expected for a portion of town, chances are that real estate values will increase (or they have already increased based upon investor expectations).

Consider demographics in conjunction with the forces of supply and demand. When there are more people, there will be greater general demand for homes and many goods and services. The demographics in a certain area will determine the demand for specific types of products. For example, if the trending population in a certain neighborhood consists primarily of high-income-earning individuals, these people will most likely want higher cost homes and entertainment (i.e., gourmet restaurants, theaters, etc.). For lower income areas, more people may be forced to rent homes rather than buy and the demand for lower cost goods and services will be higher (i.e., movie theaters, franchised restaurants, etc.).

Specific demographics of an area can translate into lower or higher property values. Rents for homes and businesses will also be determined by demand and affordability. High-end businesses can usually pay more rent, but the success of such a business is contingent upon the volume and type of clients that can be attracted. Therefore, you would expect lower rents and lower property values in poorer sections of town than when compared to wealthier areas. Consider current and expected demographic trends before investing in properties.

THE PATH OF GROWTH

When a particular block, town, or city has favorable projected demographics and population increases, the surrounding areas are often considered to be in "the path of growth." As available land becomes scarce and congested, the normal building cycle often continues the growth trend into the surrounding areas. For example, a particular county may be experiencing significant demand in excess of supply, which will result in appreciating real estate values. Real estate investors and builders may begin acquiring land and building residential and commercial structures in adjacent counties. These outlying areas may offer attractive profits to real estate investors who are willing to offer more affordable residential and commercial properties and bet on continued growth.

The advantages and disadvantages of investing within the path of growth can be seen around popular cities such as Phoenix and Las Vegas. Both cities have had strong job markets and favorable overall demographics, which has led to significant demand for residential housing. The more people and houses, the more commercial space needed to support their shopping and other service needs. The more jobs, the more demand for office and other forms of commercial space for employers. All of these factors raise real estate values and make property ownership less affordable for many individuals and businesses.

As more and more jobs were created and more and more people moved to work in Phoenix and Las Vegas, the surrounding areas continued to be developed and expanded further and further out. People wanting short commutes to these cities were forced to pay high prices and rents for homes. People willing to endure longer commutes were able to pay lower prices and rents for housing. Businesses wanting higher traffic flows of more affluent consumers to sell specialized products needed to pay higher rents for space in downtown areas. Those businesses selling more generalized products could locate in the suburbs and pay significantly lower rents. Many large communities outside of Phoenix and Las Vegas were once desert land. These properties were in the path of growth and at some point their values began to appreciate rapidly.

The development patterns of Phoenix and Las Vegas were typical for areas experiencing rapid growth and outward expansion during the recent housing market boom. These are desirable cities with favorable long-term demographics and such expansions provided excellent investment opportunities for a number of years. However, these two cities are also examples of how overdevelopment and greed can lead to unfortunate outcomes.

Properties that appear to be on a path of growth can lead to a path of stagnation and monetary loss. As markets continued to overheat, Phoenix and Las Vegas real estate developers and investors ignored the fundamentals of rising real estate values, unaffordable homes, and increasing supply.

Land values that have fallen the most dramatically during recent years (in some cases 50% or more) are the ones furthest away from the major metropolitan cities because projected paths of growth have ceased and come to a standstill. Properties that were expected to be developed in a number of months are now being placed on hold for many years. Most of these properties will change hands at substantial discounts as owners can no longer afford debt payments and investment strategies are no longer viable. When seeking to invest within an expected path of growth, make sure that the demographics are sustainable and make sense.

A FAVORABLE PRESENCE

You have heard it before and you will hear it again—location is one of the keys to real estate value. I cannot argue with this notion and most of the points discussed so far support the attractiveness or unattractiveness of a property's location. For example, a location is desirable when there is strong local demand and favorable demographics.

It is obvious that people want to live in warm, friendly, and safe neighborhoods. As patrons, they also want to frequent clean, well-maintained, and well-lit establishments. The types and conditions of surrounding residences and businesses will help drive the value of the properties within the same community. For example, high-paying tenants will be unwilling to rent homes or commercial space next to a strip club or biker bar. Sometimes the uses and pricing of certain real estate is limited by its neighbors.

The traffic count surrounding a commercial property is another key consideration. The more people driving by your property, the more income it can produce and the greater its value. The flow of traffic is also important. If you own a coffee shop, you most likely want the majority of the morning traffic to run past your site and not on the opposite side of the street.

Property accessibility is another consideration. When I lived in Florida, there was a lane divider that prevented me from entering the closest gas station to my home and I was forced to go out of my way to enter the property. I therefore chose another brand and location for my gasoline and convenience store purchases. Ease of access from a road to a site is important.

Other major, neighboring tenants can add significantly to a property's traffic flow. For example, a large grocery store in the same shopping center will attract customers. These consumers may visit other nearby shops for movies, restaurants, electronics, coffee, etc. The more desirable such an "anchor tenant," the more traffic that will be generated. Higher rents can be charged for greater traffic, which leads to a higher property value.

CASH FLOW

The level of cash flow produced by a property can be a key determinant of the property's overall value and its potential value and it can greatly enhance an investor's profitability. For income-producing property, such as an apartment building or retail store that is leased by the property owner to tenants, cash flow and expected appreciation in value determine overall profitability.

When holding a noncash-flowing property, you are betting solely on appreciation to determine profitability. Cash flow generated from a property in the form of rent helps to cover the payments associated with any debt financing. It also helps to pay for any insurance, maintenance, and repair costs. Such expenses must be paid by other sources for properties that cannot be rented or that are vacant.

The quality of the cash flow is also a key consideration. Properties leased to strong tenants that have little risk of defaulting on their leases have greater value than those leased to unproven and weaker tenants. In addition, longer term leases with favorable rent structures often have greater value than shorter term leases. However, a long-term lease with a below-market lease rate and no or weak rent escalation clauses can significantly reduce a property's value. In such cases, the owner cannot remove the tenant and is forced to accept lower rents for the remaining term of the lease.

We will talk about the most common ways to value real estate in a later chapter. We will also cover the "time value of money" and why cash inflows today have a much more dramatic effect than the same cash inflows received sometime in the future. For now, just realize that cash that can be generated from a property can help to cover costs and increase the total return that a property provides to an investor. For example, land owned and held for future sale can become more profitable if leased to farmers each year until the time of sale. A property that has a tenant paying $1,000 a month rent when other tenants will pay $2,000 a month for the same property should be valued assuming the lower rent for the existing tenant's remaining lease term and then higher rent for the following years. Some investors will seek properties with below-market rents or with high vacancies and try to improve cash flow by charging higher rents and finding additional tenants.

INTEREST RATES

Generally, lower interest rates mean lower mortgage payments by real estate investors and home buyers. When loan payments are relatively low, more home buyers can qualify to purchase a house which increases demand for residential real estate. Greater demand leads to higher prices.

Lower interest rates also help to increase the net cash flow generated from a property since interest expense is reduced by lower mortgage payments. Greater cash flow often leads to higher real estate values for many types of properties. This also means that investors can pay more for properties and still meet their minimum profitability targets.

When interest rates are low on comparable investments, the returns demanded by real estate investors are usually relatively low as well. As interest rates rise on alternative investments such as government and corporate bonds, real estate investors will usually demand higher expected returns from their real estate investments.

History has shown that real estate prices have risen in low- and high-interest-rate environments, so I am not implying that rising interest rates will always mean lower real estate appreciation. However, governments lower interest rates to spur economic growth and increase interest rates to slow economic growth. Normally, low-interest-rate environments are intended to cause greater future growth and rapidly appreciating real estate markets often take place during times of low interest rates.

SUMMARY

When considering what drives real estate values, the topics referenced above probably seem pretty simple. But making money in real estate often involves evaluating such characteristics and trends and taking a chance on the future. Prudent real estate investors need to study and understand the directions that value drivers are heading. Sometimes people just take a chance and get lucky. But the better investors leave less to chance by developing rational predictions and improving their odds of making money in all markets. Never just buy a property to follow the crowd. Take the time to research the expected value drivers and make your decisions based on proper planning and a logical investment strategy.

Chapter 3

THE ADVANTAGES OF POOLED CAPITAL

There are many ways that investors can join together and commingle their funds in order to become a greater force when investing in real estate. This may be done through the grouping of a few investors that have existing relationships with one another or on a much greater scale whereby each investor represents a small fraction of the total investment. This chapter focuses on the benefits of pooling investor cash or "equity" to enhance portfolio diversification, increase purchasing power and cost synergies, and expand the universe of investment opportunities.

POOLED CAPITAL EXAMPLES

Pooled capital can take many forms. On the largest scale, the most common format is a REIT. Congress created the legislative structure for REITs in 1960 to allow small investors to invest in large-scale, income-producing real estate. REITs use pooled capital from many investors to purchase income-producing real estate and to make loans to borrowers secured by real estate. Most REITs are traded on major stock exchanges. Buying and selling stock on a national stock exchange is much easier, faster, and cheaper than trying to buy and sell individual properties. Hence, REITs have converted real estate from illiquid to liquid assets.

REITs raise capital through the sale of their stock to institutional and individual investors. They also raise money by issuing debt to investors and by borrowing funds from banks and other lenders. By purchasing stock in a REIT, people can gain ownership of numerous large investment properties that would normally be far too expensive for an individual investor.

REITs can raise millions and even billions of dollars of capital. Having this financial strength and size allows REITs to purchase large properties such as hotels, retail shopping centers, warehouses, and office buildings. Many REITs focus on a specific real estate sector, which allows investors to choose which

REITs to invest in based upon their specific investment targets and strategies. For example, one REIT may focus solely on hotel and resort properties, while another may focus on apartment buildings or self-storage facilities. REITs have experienced management teams that are able to manage all aspects of owning multiple, large-scale properties across the country and even world.

Many companies choose to be a REIT because of the tax advantages associated with such a tax and legal structure. As long as a REIT meets certain ongoing requirements such as holding a minimum amount of real estate and paying the majority of its earnings to its shareholders each year, there are significant tax benefits. Most corporations are taxed by the government on any profits earned. In addition, the shareholders or owners of the corporation are also taxed when the company pays them any dividends. This form of double taxation can be avoided under a REIT structure because REITs do not have to pay taxes on the income they earn. Rather, only a REIT's shareholders are taxed on REIT earnings as they receive dividend payments.

There are many other forms of pooled capital. Mutual funds are another example of entities that raise money from many investors and benefit from economies of scale and general synergies. Some real estate mutual funds actively purchase properties, while others invest in companies like REITs that own and manage real estate.

Many private real estate ventures are structured as partnerships or limited liability companies. These entities are often created by a real estate investor or developer to pursue a specific purpose. Such activities could include a construction project, a land speculation venture, and the buying of a portfolio of properties to be leased. By pooling capital from many investors, enough cash can be raised to complete a specific project or accomplish a particular objective.

THE BENEFITS OF DIVERSIFICATION

By pooling capital, investors are able to group together and purchase a greater number of properties. This strategy can provide investors with greater diversification, which can reduce the amount of risk associated with a particular portfolio of properties.

Assume that a real estate investor has $50,000 to invest. If we assume that he can borrow 75% of a property's value from a bank, this means that he can afford a $200,000 property. In today's market, $200,000 would most likely buy a single-family home or a condominium.

When owning one or just a few properties, real estate investors can become poorly diversified. In such cases, investors can become overly dependent on the performance of one investment. If there is extended vacancy time or a large unexpected expense arises, the profitability of a property can decline significantly. The same is true if a local or regional recession takes place. Perhaps the primary employer in an area downsizes or goes out of business or moves its operations. For a variety of reasons, the supply of real estate in a given area can rise to vastly exceed the current level of demand. All of these possibilities support the basic investment principle of diversification.

Now let us assume that the same investor has nine friends who each have $50,000 to invest. Combined, these ten investors have a total of $500,000 in cash. Assuming that the same 75% bank financing is available, together these investors can buy a portfolio of properties worth $2 million. With this much buying power, the investor group can achieve substantially greater diversification.

Diversification provides investors with lower risk and the ability to better weather real estate cycles. By owning properties in different cities or states, geographic diversification is achieved. Layering lease terms so that multiple tenants do not vacate in a similar time frame provides cash flow diversification. Having different tenants operating different types of businesses provides industry diversification. When one or more properties are vacant and noncash flowing, other properties can be performing well and helping to cover total portfolio debt and maintenance costs. For a development project, having some properties in the construction phase and others in rental or sales stages can provide project diversification.

I devoted an entire chapter in my first book to diversification because it is such an important fundamental principle, and it pertains to all types of investing.

INCREASED PURCHASING POWER AND COST SYNERGIES

The pooling of capital allows investors to band together to make more substantial purchases and control much larger pieces of property. In addition, better efficiencies can be achieved by owning a larger portfolio of properties, which can result in significantly lower costs and greater investor profitability.

We have discussed how combining investor capital can allow a venture to purchase larger properties and a greater number of properties when compared to individual investment alternatives. This increased purchasing power allows investors to own and control real estate investments that would normally be out of reach. When combined with borrowings from banks and other lenders as discussed in the next chapter, investor purchasing power is magnified.

Depending on the extent of your real estate investing and the level of your involvement, the infrastructure needed to manage a portfolio of real estate investments efficiently and prudently will vary. For example, managing one or two single-family homes should not normally take too much effort. However, managing a large shopping center or a construction project requires specific expertise and resources.

Often times, the same amount of management expertise and time is needed to oversee portfolios of varying size. Costs such as personnel, office space, supplies, property management and accounting systems, tax and legal services, and other expenses often associated with successful real estate management and oversight can be spread over a larger number of investments. When properties can be added to an existing management structure without materially increasing total expenses, synergies can be generated that lower investor costs.

Lower costs to an investor can be generated through fee discounts from a property management firm as the investor continues to purchase more properties. This can apply to both residential and commercial investments. By investing with others, the greater purchasing power achieved can create greater interest from property management firms and cause them to be more aggressive in bidding their services. Often times, investors can benefit from the significant real estate development and management expertise of one or more partners running a particular investment venture.

EXPAND THE UNIVERSE OF OPPORTUNITIES

Combining investor capital opens the doors to many additional opportunities that might otherwise be unavailable to individual investors. For example, certain property types are generally too expensive for most individuals. In addition, owning such large properties individually can easily result in poor portfolio diversification, which can increase an investor's risk profile.

Consider property types such as hotels, warehouses, office buildings, shopping centers, ski resorts, and marinas. Without pooled capital, the vast majority of investors would be unable to own these types of assets. This would dramatically reduce the universe of investment opportunities for real estate investors.

I have always found more profitable business opportunities to exist for people and entities having substantial available capital. For example, usually properties being auctioned by lenders or local governments have minimum bidding requirements. Most individuals are unaware of the majority of real estate investment opportunities because they are shown to and negotiated with people and entities that have substantial capital. When sellers know that you have reliable and sufficient access to funds, they take you more seriously.

By having access to pooled capital investments such as REITs, mutual funds, and other managed vehicles, small investors can own a portion of a large-scale shopping center or a full-service hotel. They can spread their real estate investments among a variety of sectors. Individuals can also invest in international real estate markets and allow experienced management teams to oversee foreign currency, legal, and political risks. By having such a broad range of opportunities, investors can earn higher returns, and at the same time receive substantial diversification and risk reduction benefits.

SUMMARY

The intent of this chapter is to highlight the benefits of aggregating investor capital in order to magnify investor purchasing power. Doing so can provide substantial diversification benefits, which can significantly increase profitability through a broader universe of investment choices and lower cost structures.

The following chapter discusses the benefits of leverage and the use of other people's money to enhance investment returns. Pooled investor capital combined with a borrowing ability that can often increase investor purchasing power by two to three times creates one of the most basic but powerful investment strategies used continuously by most successful real estate investors.

Chapter 4

THE BENEFITS AND RISKS OF LEVERAGE

The term "leverage" refers to an investor's ability to borrow against a portion of the purchase price or value of one or more pieces of collateral. By borrowing cash from a bank or other lender in order to purchase a piece of real estate, you have essentially used someone else's money to increase the size of your investment. In addition, by borrowing at attractive interest rates, you can greatly enhance the profitability of your invested capital by making money on the money that you have borrowed.

THE ABILITY TO BORROW

Lenders are usually willing to lend up to 90% of a property's value. The dollar amount will vary based upon the specific collateral and, if needed, the strength of any entities or persons guaranteeing the repayment of the debt. Lenders will find certain types of properties more risky than others. For example, when seeking a loan to purchase a property that is leased to a restaurant operator, many lenders become skeptical since so many restaurants are unsuccessful. When requesting to borrow against vacant land, many lenders may pass on the idea or only lend 40–60% of the value. However, borrowing to buy a small retail shopping center with long leases to strong tenants may become much easier and lenders may be willing to provide closer to 90% financing.

Lenders often feel more comfortable lending larger sums of money and for longer periods of time when real estate is the underlying collateral. This is because real estate is a tangible asset that tends to hold and increase its value over time. In addition, the capital markets have become very efficient in financing many types of real estate loans which has lowered the costs to borrowers and streamlined the borrowing process.

Finding a lender that is willing to lend you money to purchase and own real estate is often much easier than when attempting to borrow using other types of collateral. When compared to collateral such as stocks and bonds, automobiles, and other consumer products, real estate can be a much more attractive source of repayment to a lender.

YOU NEED LEVERAGE TO COMPETE

Real estate markets are very competitive. There are always billions of dollars of available capital seeking profitable real estate investments. Most of this money is in the form of pooled investor capital held by large companies and funds. These types of investment vehicles range in size and scope. Some are small and focus only on local or regional property acquisitions and ownership. Others are much larger and have national and international investment objectives. Depending upon your investment strategies, you may be competing with these entities and/or with individual real estate investors. For example, when looking to buy single-family rental homes, you will be bidding against other individual real estate investors, as well as home buyers seeking new residences. If you are looking to acquire a large shopping center, your primary competitors will most likely be real estate companies and funds.

In many circumstances, a real estate investment is not worth considering unless a substantial amount of leverage is used. Without leverage, the profitability of investing in real estate becomes substantially lower. This is because of the level of competition you are facing. Because everyone else is forecasting the profitability of a particular investment based upon the expected use of leverage, unless you are assuming similar financing, you will be at a severe disadvantage.

THE BENEFITS OF LEVERAGE

As mentioned, leverage can significantly enhance the profitability of an investment. By using dollars provided by a lender, you can make money on the money that you invest and on the money that was lent to you. The trick is finding investments that will earn higher returns than the cost of the debt you are borrowing. For example, assume that you find a real estate investment that earns 10% per year and that you can borrow 75% of the money needed to purchase the property at an annual interest rate of 7%. You will need to invest your own cash to cover 25% of the purchase price for which you will earn a 10% annual return. In addition, your lender will be providing you with 75% of the purchase price that will also earn 10% per year. However, you are only paying your lender 7% for the borrowed funds. This means that you are earning 3% each year on the money that you borrowed.

Leverage allows investors to make larger purchases and obtain control of larger assets. For example, assume that you find a property that costs $1,000,000. You feel that this is the deal of a lifetime, but you have nowhere close to $1,000,000 in cash. But if your local bank is willing to lend you 80% of the purchase price, you have now reduced your cash down payment needs from $1,000,000 to only $200,000. This is still a lot of money, but you have made a great reduction in your cash needs through the use of leverage. Now assume that you have four friends and each of you is willing and able to invest $40,000. You have now pooled capital and have the buying power to control a $1,000,000 piece of property.

There are tax benefits associated with the use of leverage. Interest expense on most properties is tax deductible. Just like when you deduct repair and maintenance costs related to your real estate investments, you can also deduct the interest payments that you make to your lender. This tax benefit provided by the government essentially reduces your actual cost of borrowing. The following formula illustrates this point:

After Tax Interest Rate = (Before Tax Interest Rate) × (1 − Borrower's Tax Rate)

When a lender charges interest on a loan, if the interest is tax deductible, then the rate of interest that you are really paying will be substantially lower. Let us use an example to test this formula. Assume that a bank lends you money to purchase a property at an annual interest rate of 7%. If your tax bracket is 25%, to determine the after tax cost of interest on the loan, we would use the formula as follows:

After Tax Interest Rate = (7%) × (1 − 25%)

After Tax Interest Rate = 5.25%

This means that you are actually paying an after tax interest rate on this loan of only 5.25%. Tax deductibility is a key benefit associated with the use of leverage that individuals and entities rely upon when making real estate investments.

EXAMPLES OF THE BENEFITS OF LEVERAGE

As discussed, the use of leverage can enhance the profitability of an investment by allowing an investor to make money on the funds borrowed from a lender and from the tax deductibility of interest payments. In addition, leverage allows investors to buy and control larger pieces of property.

Let us look at an example to illustrate the benefits of leverage. Assume that an investor identifies a plot of vacant land that he thinks is undervalued and that will significantly appreciate over the next five years. Also assume that the investor is presented with the two financing alternatives to purchase the property that are identified in Table 4.1. In Scenario 1, he can purchase the land for cash at a price of $200,000. In Scenario 2, the investor can purchase the same piece of land using $40,000 of his own money and $160,000 that he receives as a loan from a bank.

To determine which financing option is best, we need to look at the expected profitability of each scenario. Let us assume that the investor expects the property to appreciate in value on average by 8% per year, and after five years, he plans to sell the property for a profit, take his cash proceeds, and pay any taxes due. Let us also assume that in Scenario 2 the investor can borrow $160,000 from a bank at an interest rate of 7% per year.

When comparing Scenario 2 to Scenario 1, we realize a few key differences. Scenario 2 requires that the investor have only $40,000 to purchase the property versus the $200,000 of cash required in Scenario 1. This is a very important consideration because most people do not have $200,000 in cash. However, by

Table 4.1
No Leverage versus Leverage Scenarios

	Scenario 1		Scenario 2	
	0% Debt		80% Debt	
Land purchase price	$	200,000	$	200,000
Debt financing from a bank		–		160,000
Investor's equity (down payment)	$	200,000	$	40,000
Land value in 5 years	$	293,866	$	293,866
(assumes 8% appreciation each year)				
Cost of property		(200,000)		(200,000)
Increase in value	$	93,866	$	93,866
Loan payments at 7% for 5 years		–		(56,000)
Gross profit	$	93,866	$	37,866
Income taxes		(14,080)		(5,680)
(assumes 15% capital gains tax)				
Total after-tax profit	$	79,786	$	32,186
Return on investor's equity		39.9%		80.5%

using bank financing to purchase the majority of the property, the investor will need to repay the loan to the bank with interest. He needs to ensure that either the property generates enough cash to make these payments or that he has other means to do so. Another consideration is that the interest on the bank loan in Scenario 2 is tax deductible. This means that while the investor is paying the bank an interest rate of 7%, the interest payments are reducing the investor's tax burden and he is paying a lower effective interest rate on the bank loan.

As indicated in Table 4.1, if the investor chooses Scenario 1, he can earn $79,786 in after-tax profit, while if he chooses to finance the investment under the terms of Scenario 2, he would earn only $32,186. If this was our only consideration, one might choose the terms of Scenario 1 and pay cash for the property. However, under Scenario 1 the investor would need to invest $200,000 of his own cash to earn $79,786 over a five-year period. This would result in a five-year return of 39.9% on his initial investment ($79,786/$200,000 = 39.9%). But if the bank financing in Scenario 2 was used to purchase the property, the investor would need to invest only $40,000 of his own money in order to earn $32,186, which is a five-year return of 80.5% on his initial investment. I would certainly take an 80.5% return over a 39.9% return!

Scenario 2 provides such a higher return on invested cash because of the use of financial leverage. By using this financing structure, the investor would make money not only on his $40,000 down payment but also on the bank's money that he invested.

I want to show you a similar example to further stress the benefits of leverage. Table 4.1 showed somewhat of an "apples to oranges" comparison between Scenarios 1 and 2. The reason is that when comparing these two scenarios, the investor is making a different down payment amount ($200,000 in Scenario 1 and only $40,000 in Scenario 2). Assuming the investor had $200,000 in cash before making his decision to use the financing structure in Scenario 2, he would still have an extra $160,000 of cash to further invest. This is not reflected in Table 4.1.

Table 4.2 shows a similar analysis as Table 4.1, but both the two scenarios in Table 4.2 assume that the same amount of the investor's cash is invested. Let us assume that the investor has $200,000 of cash that he wants to invest. Under Scenario 1, he can purchase the land for $200,000 without leverage and he will have fully invested all of his cash. In Scenario 2, assume that the investor wants to use leverage to maximize his earnings and he wants to invest the same $200,000 of his own cash.

Because the investor is investing his entire $200,000 in cash and using 80% leverage in the form of bank financing under Scenario 2, he is able to buy $1,000,000 worth of land. So let us assume that he buys the first plot of land for $200,000 and buys four other plots for $200,000 each. Now the investor is fully employing his cash and maximizing his return through the use of leverage.

As shown at the bottom of Table 4.2, the investor is still earning the same returns as in Table 4.1 (39.9% in Scenario 1 and 80.5% in Scenario 2). However,

Table 4.2
No Leverage versus Leverage Scenarios with Equal Equity Investments

	Scenario 1		Scenario 2	
	0% Debt		80% Debt	
Land purchase price	$	200,000	$	1,000,000
Debt financing		–		800,000
Investor's equity (down payment)	$	200,000	$	200,000
Land value in 5 years	$	293,866	$	1,469,328
(assumes 8% appreciation each year)				
Cost of property		(200,000)		(1,000,000)
Increase in value	$	93,866	$	469,328
Loan payments at 7% for 5 years		–		(280,000)
Gross profit	$	93,866	$	189,328
Income taxes		(14,080)		(28,399)
(assumes 15% capital gains tax)				
Total after-tax profit	$	79,786	$	160,929
Return on investor's equity		39.9%		80.5%

because the investor is now investing his full $200,000 in Scenario 2, he is now reaping the benefits of making the larger investment. In Table 4.2, the investor invests $200,000 of cash under each scenario. The difference of making $160,929 versus $79,786 is due to leverage.

The benefits of leverage shown above can generate the same results with any size investment and the principles are exactly the same. The basic assumption is that you are borrowing money at a cheaper rate than you are earning.

THE RISKS OF LEVERAGE

While leverage can greatly enhance the profitability of an investment, it clearly increases an investor's risk exposure. Problems result when an investment is not earning a return that is greater than the cost of the money borrowed. For example, if you borrow money from a bank at 7% per year, but your investment earns something less than 7% annually, then you are losing money on the money that you borrowed. In such a circumstance, you are earning a low or negative return on your own cash investment, but you also have to cover the losses on the bank's money.

Table 4.3 uses similar assumptions as in Table 4.2 except that the profitability of the investment is lower. In Table 4.3, the land purchased under each scenario is assumed to increase in value by only 3% per year (versus 8% in Tables 4.1 and 4.2), which is substantially lower than the 7% interest rate that the investor is paying to the bank.

As can be seen in Table 4.3, the use of leverage can be dangerous. When the return on investment is lower than the cost of borrowing, profits can be greatly reduced and losses can result. In such cases, an investor that chose not to use leverage would be in a better position. Had he chosen to use solely his own cash to finance his investment in Scenario 1, he would still have a positive five-year return of 13.5%. While this is a poor return for a five-year investment that averages only 2.7% per year, it is far better than the loss that resulted by leveraging a much larger investment under Scenario 2.

When making a larger investment through the use of leverage in Scenario 2, the investment results in a substantial loss. In this case, the investor would have lost over half of his original investment of $200,000 because he would need to repay the bank its full loan amount. Scenario 2 in Table 4.3 also assumes that the investor can use a tax credit of $18,109 to reduce his loss, which is not always allowable under the tax guidelines. If unable to do so, his losses would become even greater.

Table 4.3 illustrates one of the many ways that investors get into trouble through real estate investing. The more money you borrow, the greater the risks when the investment does not earn an adequate return. Had we assumed only 50% leverage in Scenario 2 instead of 80%, the loss would have been substantially lower. However, the same principles would apply in Tables 4.1 and 4.2 under favorable land appreciation scenarios. If we had assumed lower leverage in these scenarios, then the investor profits would have been substantially lower as well.

Leverage increases investor profitability when an investment earns a greater return than the cost of debt, but it also increases investor losses when the investment earns a return that is lower than the cost of debt. We will talk about ways to find favorable investments and avoid selling at a loss in other chapters.

Table 4.3

No Leverage versus Leverage Scenarios with Equal Equity Investments: 3% Annual Appreciation in Land Values

	Scenario 1		Scenario 2	
	0% Debt		80% Debt	
Land purchase price	$	200,000	$	1,000,000
Debt financing		–		800,000
Investor's equity (down payment)	$	200,000	$	200,000
Land value in 5 years *(assumes 3% appreciation each year)*	$	231,855	$	1,159,274
Cost of property		(200,000)		(1,000,000)
Increase in value	$	31,855	$	159,274
Loan payments at 7% for 5 years		–		(280,000)
Gross profit/(loss)	$	31,855		($120,726)
Income taxes/(tax credit) *(assumes 15% capital gains tax)*		(4,778)		18,109
Total after-tax profit	$	27,077		($102,617)
Return on investor's equity		13.5%		(51.3%)

Another risk associated with the use of leverage is the need to make ongoing payments to your lender. Some lenders require monthly, quarterly, or annual payments that usually include interest and some amount of principal repayment. Other loans require borrowers to fund interest reserve accounts that a lender will use to cover borrower payments for a specific period of time. Some loans may allow the borrower to repay all interest and principal at the time of loan maturity.

Real estate investors must plan ahead and ensure that they will be able to make scheduled payments to their lenders. This includes both periodic payments and the repayment of principal at the time of a loan's maturity. Such planning requires consideration of the expected and the unexpected.

As a repercussion of the current residential housing market deterioration, I have seen numerous real estate developers lose their land investments because they could no longer make their scheduled interest and principal payments. Many of these people had invested millions of dollars of their own and other people's money to help purchase these properties. But when the market turned downward, they did not have the financial resources to ride out the market cycle. The same thing has happened and continues to happen with investors that bought single-family homes and can no longer make their mortgage payments. They expected to buy and sell quickly in a favorable market. Many of these borrowers signed personal guarantees to cover any shortfall between a property's value and the dollars owed to their lenders. The better real estate investors prepare for the unexpected and ensure that they will have adequate means to make their payments under varying circumstances. We will talk more about choosing an appropriate financing structure in a later chapter.

SUMMARY

The benefits and risks of leverage apply to all kinds of real estate investments, including the ownership of a personal residence, rental properties, land speculation ventures, and construction projects. The vast majority of real estate projects that I have seen and been involved with have utilized some degree of leverage. The exact amount of leverage used is often limited by lenders depending on the specific collateral. Other times, investors choose a lower amount of leverage in order to reduce project risk in return for lower expected profitability. But often times, real estate investors will take as much leverage as a lender is willing to provide.

When discussing the risks of leverage, my intent was not to scare investors and deter the use of leverage. Rather, I just want readers to understand the potential upsides and downsides associated with borrowed funds. I am personally a strong supporter of leverage and the many benefits it provides. Hopefully as you continue reading the upcoming chapters, you will gain more comfort and knowledge regarding the ways to mitigate the risks associated with leverage and investing in real estate.

Chapter 5

BE PATIENT AND MAINTAIN HOLDING POWER

As mentioned, real estate is often a very illiquid asset. This means that it usually takes a substantial period of time to consummate a sale of one or more properties without significantly discounting the sales price. There are also many contingencies associated with real estate dealings that can cause a sales contract to be withdrawn or void. In addition, there are large transaction costs involved when buying and selling properties, including Realtor commissions, taxes, and title insurance.

All of the factors above make investing in real estate for the short term more difficult and less likely. Most real estate purchases and activities should be viewed as mid- to long-term investments. If you have an upcoming need for cash, you should consider investing the funds in short-term bank products or money market or bond funds. Do not plan to invest cash into real estate and expect to be able to receive your money back with little notice or lead time.

Purchasing the stock of a REIT is probably the most liquid form of real estate investing. But in many regards, investing in REIT stocks is just like buying the common stock of any other company listed on a major stock exchange and common stock investments are risky. Just because REITs allow investors to buy and sell their common stock within seconds does not mean that REIT stocks should be viewed as short-term investments or used to park money for short periods of time.

Most common stock and other equity investments provide investors with greater expected returns over the long-term when compared to more conservative investment alternatives (i.e., corporate and government bonds). But as a trade-off for greater expected long-term profitability, these instruments often encompass significant risk and price volatility during short periods of time. This means that if you buy the common stock of a REIT and then decide that you need your money back a month later, the price volatility associated with such an equity investment may lead to substantial losses. When seeking short-term investment options, less volatile and less risky investment products such as money market accounts would be much more suitable.

WHEN MARKETS TURN UGLY

Real estate markets go through cycles. Under normal market conditions, supply is similar to demand and real estate markets gradually increase in value at a pace comparable or somewhat better than a country's overall rate of inflation. However, markets can overheat when demand significantly outpaces supply for extended periods of time. These cycles can be local, regional, or even more national. The reasons for rapid price increases in a certain area can vary, but generally there tends to be strong demand and limited supply. Sometimes such demand is justified and supportable by demographics and other factors. Other times it is not and a correction and market decline is inevitable.

The most recent run-up in housing prices during the early and mid-2000s was driven primarily by loose lending standards, real estate speculators, and a general misconception that home prices could continue rising at double-digit rates for long periods of time. Buyers with poor credit, low incomes, and low or no down payments were wrongly able to obtain home mortgage loans. Under more prudent lending standards, many of these buyers should not have been able to qualify.

Strong housing demand attracted all kinds of real estate investors that began buying single-family homes with the intent of reselling them quickly for a profit. Many of these investors had no rational investment strategy nor should they have qualified for the financing that they received.

In addition to the lower credit standards that lenders were employing, a variety of aggressive loan products were being used to help borrowers with weaker credit qualify for mortgage loans. Examples include adjustable or "floating rate" loans, interest-only loans, and loans with initially low "teaser rates."

Interest rates in the United States have remained historically low during the 2000s which has generally helped to increase the number of qualified home buyers. This has allowed home buyers and investors to borrow relatively cheaply. The lower the interest rate on your loan, the larger the payment that you can afford and the bigger the house that you can buy. This is beneficial for home buyers when such financing is used correctly and not abused. When the interest rate on your loan is fixed for a long period, you do not have the risk of your payment increasing substantially over time as interest rates rise.

But normally floating rates of interest are lower than fixed rates of interest because a lender is taking less risk with a floating rate loan. If interest rates rise and a bank is forced to pay its depositors higher rates of interest on certificates of deposit and savings accounts, it can offset this higher cost by having floating rate loans to its borrowers. As interest rates rise on deposit accounts, so do the payments made by borrowers to the bank on floating rate loans. However, when banks provide 15- and 30-year fixed rate loans to borrowers, they run the risk of paying higher and higher interest rates to their depositors while receiving the same fixed rates of interest on their loans. In addition, floating rate loans are often much shorter in term, which also leads to lower risk for a lender and more risk for a borrower.

During such aggressive lending environments, home buyers with low incomes can more easily qualify for home loans when using adjustable rate loans versus fixed rate loans because the initial floating rates of interest are usually lower. This is what fueled the real estate bubble that burst in 2008. In addition, to magnify the problems, many lenders were offering loans with even lower initial interest rates that had scheduled reset dates sometime in the fairly near future. These teaser rates result in huge payment increases once the reset dates are reached. Other loans did not require any principal payments for a certain period of time. As these interest-only loans reset and principal repayments are required, the payments required by borrowers also greatly increase.

At the time of this writing, the effects of these aggressive lending policies and loan products have emerged, continued to worsen, and led to devastating consequences. People continue to lose their homes and foreclosure properties for sale are dominating many markets. Such discounted prices and adverse perceptions are leading to dramatic declines in housing values, which has pushed the entire country into recession and caused a global financial crisis that can only be compared to the Great Depression. Home loans and securities backed by home loans have resulted in losses of hundreds of billions of dollars for banks and other lenders. Leading financial institutions are filing bankruptcy and being forcefully acquired at shockingly low prices or taken over or rescued by federal governments.

The 2008 downturn in residential housing is an extreme example of how markets can overheat and turn unfavorable for lengthy periods of time. The pain associated with such deteriorating market conditions has many rippling effects. There is a chain of real estate investors that leads to the eventual construction and sale of a single-family home. Land owners have been taking tremendous losses. Large and small home-building companies have been writing off hundreds of millions of dollars and public home builder stocks are at dramatic lows. Many of these companies have ceased operations.

The commercial real estate markets have held up relatively well during the recent residential housing market debacle. However, there are clear signs that this market has peaked and declines in value are imminent. The overall severity of such a downturn will be contingent upon the strength of the general economy. However, whether there is a significant downturn in 2009, the following year, or five years from now, prudent real estate investors must realize that commercial real estate markets also move in cycles.

THE NEED FOR HOLDING POWER

Holding power refers to an investor's ability to maintain control and ownership of a property for an extended period of time. This ability becomes most important during declining real estate markets. Such poorly performing real estate cycles can quickly cause investors, banks, and other providers of capital to become nervous and skeptical and want their money back as quickly as possible. These are the worst times to be forced to sell a property and such circumstances can lead investors to voluntarily or involuntarily give up control of their properties and lose large sums of money.

In order to have and maintain proper holding power, an investor needs to have the willingness and the ability to hold a property or investment for extended periods of time. The willingness pertains to the mentality of the investor. Many people panic when markets turn ugly and sell their investments at unfavorable times and at deep discounts. Sometimes such a strategy can make sense, but other times your loss is someone else's gain.

Having the ability to hold an investment through both the good times and bad is based more on an investor's capital position. If you paid cash for a property and you do not have an immediate need for your funds, then you probably have long-term holding power. But as mentioned, most real estate investors employ some degree of leverage when buying and owning real estate investments.

People that take out loans with short terms or with scheduled payment increases that they cannot afford do not have proper holding power. Banks and other lenders are clearly responsible for a portion of the blame associated with the recently inflated residential real estate markets. There is no doubt that many of their borrowers should not have qualified for financing. However, a prudent real estate investor needs to evaluate his financing options carefully and ensure that he has adequate holding power through favorable and unfavorable markets.

BE PATIENT AND DO NOT PANIC

Banks have a reputation for selling real estate quickly at large losses. When these financial institutions are forced to foreclose on properties held by defaulted borrowers, they become the new owner. Real estate owned by a bank ties up the bank's money and adds nothing to the bank's earnings. The main objective becomes selling the real estate as quickly as possible and reinvesting the proceeds into new loans that can help to increase profits.

The sales process for many lending institutions is often somewhat robotic. Banks will often sell a property quickly at the current market price. Remember that real estate is an illiquid asset. Under normal market conditions, it can take months to sell a property at a fair price. The faster a seller tries to sell, the more price concession that is often needed. Under unfavorable market conditions, the selling time frame can become much longer and there may be very few buyers. In fact, when markets get really bad, it seems like the only available buyers are the ones looking to take advantage of other people's misfortune. In such cases, current market price represents a huge discount.

Sometimes banks try to get rid of many properties at once through a portfolio sale. In this case, a bank may bundle a dozen or dozens of properties before marketing them for sale to real estate investors. By buying in bulk, investors can sometimes find even greater discounts because banks and other sellers want to sell many properties fairly quickly. I have recently seen several portfolios being offered at 40–50% of the appraised values used when the bank originally lent the money to the defaulted borrowers.

Banks are renowned for lacking in holding power. Their quickness to sell during all market conditions provides buyers with great opportunities. In general, banks are good lenders, but they are not good real estate investors. While they often have the ability to maintain holding power, they usually do not have the willingness.

Human behavior is often prone to panicking and following the crowd. A key separation between the skilled real estate investor and the novice is proper planning, a cool head, and logical decision making. Just because other people are avoiding the real estate markets does not mean that this is the right decision for a smart investor. Just as so many inexperienced investors buy high and sell low in the stock markets, such behavior is very common in real estate investing as well.

Make sure that you have the willingness to maintain holding power. Do not panic in unfavorable circumstances and make your decisions based upon reasonable planning and investment strategies. This is not to imply that investors should always hold properties and be unwilling to sell. This is not the case. In cyclical markets such as real estate, there are always more favorable and unfavorable times to buy and sell. Just realize that the goal of maintaining holding power is to avoid selling real estate at unfavorable times at large discounts and the willingness to have holding power is primarily a state of mind.

It is very common for individual real estate investors to have the willingness to maintain holding power, but not the ability. This problem is usually driven by insufficient capital. Ways to ensure adequate capital include obtaining financing with favorable and predictable terms, finding strong tenants with long and layered leases, and stressing investment scenarios to ensure proper cash flow during difficult times.

When obtaining financing for real estate acquisitions, make sure that the loan terms are long enough to cover the length of your investments. This is particularly important for fairly short-term investments such as construction projects and speculative ventures. Just because you plan to construct a building in 12 months and sell it to someone shortly after completion is no guarantee. Bad weather, labor shortages, design changes, and sales delays are just some of the events that can increase a project's timeline. Often it is not a problem to extend financing in good markets, but in bad markets and under changing project circumstances, lenders can become much more conservative.

In today's market, the original business plans for many land owners are no longer realistic. To find financing to build houses during a real estate depression is exceptionally difficult. In addition, to build houses when there is over ten months of home inventories on the market and a slew of bank foreclosures on the way would not be a wise decision. Most people that own land use some type of leverage to make their purchases. Often times, interest rates for raw land acquisitions can be in the low- to mid-teens. Carrying such debt for extended periods of time can quickly turn a project unprofitable.

Consider a portfolio of rental properties. These could be commercial properties leased to different retail or corporate tenants. Alternatively, an investor might own several single-family homes leased to renting tenants. Regardless of the types of properties, one way to increase holding power is to have strong tenants with layered lease maturity dates. This is one way to reduce the risk of losing too many tenants in the same time frame, which could result in a severe drain on an investor's cash flow.

Investors must also stress test their real estate investments to ensure that debt and other required payments can be afforded and that holding power can be maintained when needed. For example, if a rental property becomes vacant for an extended period of time or needs a major repair or renovation, the property owner or owners should have the resources to make the required payments. If loan payments are scheduled to increase or have the potential to increase in the future, these changes should be expected and not cause an excessive financial burden.

SUMMARY

As a real estate investor, you do not want to put yourself in a position that forces you to sell your real estate investments in order to repay debt or meet other unexpected obligations. Rather, you want to make sure that you have enough available funds to provide you with adequate holding power. We will talk more about finding and utilizing the best sources of financing and when it makes sense to sell and buy properties. For now, just realize that selling an illiquid asset quickly can result in substantial losses. And when markets turn ugly and the only available buyers are seeking deep discounts from troubled sellers, the numbers can only get worse. The skilled real estate investor plans ahead and has the willingness and the ability to maintain proper holding power.

Chapter 6

ONE PERSON'S MISFORTUNE IS ANOTHER'S FORTUNE

People that lack the willingness or the ability to maintain holding power provide numerous opportunities for other real estate investors. Just as in stock and bond markets, real estate cycles often move too far in one direction before trending back to more reasonable pricing levels. For example, it is obvious that homes selling for 40 cents on the dollar in today's depressed residential real estate market are undervalued. Anyone having the capital and initiative can make substantial profits by buying such investments and implementing a patient marketing approach or by holding the properties until market conditions improve.

Also creating great opportunities in real estate investing is the general illiquidity of real estate. Selling real estate requires considerable time and selling costs even during normal market conditions. When markets turn ugly and there are limited buyers, the swings in relative value can be even more dramatic and selling properties can take substantially longer. People that need or want to sell fast, particularly in down markets, will usually suffer a high cost for greater liquidity.

The misfortune of one real estate investor can often become a great buying opportunity for another investor. As mentioned earlier and as proven historically, when real estate markets turn ugly, millions and even billions of dollars can be lost in a declining market. However, similar profits can be earned as markets begin to rationalize, bounce back, and move upward.

WHAT CREATES A DESPERATE SELLER?

There are many reasons why a seller wants or needs to sell a particular piece of property. I usually find the residential real estate markets to be less rational than commercial real estate markets. This is mostly due to the lesser level of investment knowledge and sophistication held by the average homeowner. However, there are clearly attractive opportunities that arise in both markets.

When buyers know that you are desperate to sell, they try to take advantage of your misfortune. You will receive offers that you will find insulting and absurd. But in general I tend to take all offers seriously. I can remember having properties listed and receiving offers that were up to 30% lower than my asking price. After I countered with a selling price reduction of only a few percentage points, these potential buyers made much more realistic offers. They had been fishing for bargains and needed to know that I was serious about my asking price. Other sellers might have panicked and negotiated around a lowball offer.

When sellers have moved and their prior home is vacant and listed for sale, a sense of desperation quickly emerges and most buyers know this. When owners are making payments for mortgages, electric and water, landscaping, insurance, property taxes, etc. for their new home and their old home, most are very eager to sell quickly. In addition, there is a mental burden associated with owning a vacant property, particularly when the owner has moved to a distant location and cannot watch over it.

Many buyers will pay attention to how long a property has been listed on the market as another gauge of seller desperation. The longer a property is listed, the greater the chance that the seller is having problems finding a buyer. It costs money to "carry" a property that is not in use. This applies to commercial and residential properties. The fact that there is no tenant or owner occupying a property does not stop the monthly bills. The longer someone owns noncash-flowing and non-appreciating property, the lower the eventual net proceeds and overall profitability.

Buying opportunities often result when sellers divorce. Such an event is more likely to cause residential buying opportunities, but a divorce can also be a motivating selling factor for commercial properties as well. When businesses fail or terminate operations, buying opportunities can also result. This may be from a business owner that also owns the real estate being used to operate his business or a resulting vacancy may trigger a desired sale by a landlord.

Many sellers sell because of financial problems. There are many reasons that can cause such adverse circumstances. Loss of employment, a failed business venture, a disabling accident, or a serious illness can all lead to people wanting to sell residential and commercial real estate quickly. Perhaps someone acquired one or more properties through inheritance and he wants the cash proceeds as soon as possible. Maybe a business owner is retiring and wants to liquidate his property quickly. Often real estate owners overextend their credit and can no longer pay the debt and other expenses associated with a property.

Owners can experience financial problems when business plans do not work out as expected. For example, assume someone buys a property and plans to rent it to one or more tenants. If enough tenants cannot be found to cover the property's monthly expenses, this person may be forced to sell the property at a loss in order to eliminate the ongoing financial burden. Think about all the buyers of single-family homes during the run-up in housing prices in the early to mid-2000s. After the market stalled, many speculative investors could not sell their properties at prices even close to their purchase costs. In addition, finding tenants at rental rates sufficient to cover monthly mortgage payments in many cases was nearly impossible.

Other circumstances can result in faulty investment strategies. I witnessed a development project for fractional homes begin construction several years ago. It was expected to take three years to complete and sell about 300 ownership interests to individuals seeking vacation homes. The forecasted profit at the project's inception was approximately $15 million. But once the housing market slowed, so did the project's sales. Instead of taking three years to complete, the project is now expected to take over six years. This delay is costing millions of dollars in additional management and interest expenses. In addition, the management team has been unable to raise the sales prices for the units as much as expected. The project is now forecasted to lose about $5 million. There is also the risk that the lender on the project may foreclose on the property if the debt payments cannot be kept current.

When business plans do not materialize as expected, financial difficulties can easily arise. This is especially true when significant degrees of leverage are used to finance the development or acquisition of a property. In such cases, many buyers are unable to maintain holding power and they eventually lose control and ownership of their properties. Sometimes, this is the best outcome for the owner. Properties may have deteriorated so much in value that the best option is to allow a lender to take possession and become the new owner.

When banks or other lenders repossess the real estate that served as collateral for their loans to defaulting borrowers, the prior owner of the property loses his entire investment. This means that any investor equity invested in these properties is now lost. Such losses can provide opportunities for investors that buy properties from banks or other lenders.

The fact that defaulting investors lose their equity capital upon foreclosure allows banks and other lenders to sell these properties at a cost equal to their debt obligations and still break even. Depending on how much money was owed and how much a property may have declined in value, this initial discount can provide great buying opportunities. Additionally, because banks want to sell properties quickly, they often sell properties at a loss. Sometimes they will even provide attractive financing to buyers to help facilitate a purchase.

If banks and other regulated lenders make too many bad loans and end up with too many foreclosed properties, they can come under scrutiny from local and federal regulators. In addition, owning properties provides no earnings for lenders and earnings are what drive their stock prices and other forms of shareholder value. By selling foreclosed properties quickly, any cash received can be reinvested into income generating assets, such as new loans to performing borrowers. In addition, the less foreclosed property these entities own, the better their perceived financial condition.

SUMMARY

People and companies that own real estate can become desperate sellers for many reasons. Prudent investors keep their eyes and ears open for such opportunities. You can generally expect to see more of these buying opportunities when real estate markets are stagnant or declining. The more that supply exceeds demand and the fewer available buyers for a piece of property, the less options that are available to a seller.

There will always be owners that need or want cash quickly. And when properties have been on the market for extended periods of time, people's level of desperation tends to rise. The worse the market conditions, the more pricing concession people will be forced to provide. If you are looking to acquire properties, just be patient and wait for the better deals. With such an illiquid asset, there will always be chances to buy properties at a discount. You may not find many in certain years, but at other times such opportunities will be plentiful.

Chapter 7

VALUING REAL ESTATE

There are many ways to value real estate. However, there are three common valuation methods that are generally accepted and relied upon. Modifications to these approaches or additional approaches may be needed depending upon factors such as the specific features of a property, the terms of any leases in place, and the property's highest and best use.

Real estate appraisers rely primarily on the three valuation approaches described below. Depending on the market cycle, property type and location, varying levels of subjectivity exist when valuing real estate. I have disagreed with the values derived by many appraisers over the years (either too high or too low), but appraisals provided by certified professionals are the most credible determinations of value.

THE SALES COMPARISON APPROACH

Comparing recent sales of similar properties is the most common approach to valuing real estate when there are comparable sales available. When you are looking to buy single-family homes in a congested neighborhood, this approach works well. When you are seeking to buy an office building within an office park where virtually identical properties have been recently sold, the sales comparison approach would also be useful.

There is clearly a subjective aspect involved when deriving a property's value based upon the sales prices of other properties. In most cases, there are material differences between properties that must be considered and valued. This can result in significantly different property values by different appraisers. The greater the differences between the properties being compared, the more subjectivity that is involved. In addition, when older sales data are being used, this analysis becomes even more subjective.

Let us look at a simple example to illustrate the sales comparison approach. Table 7.1 represents some of the key criteria used in determining a value for a residential property using this method. The "subject property" is the property being valued. There are three comparable properties in the same neighborhood that have all sold within the past three months. This sales data is available to Realtors and other professionals that have access to database networks such as the Multiple Listing Service (MLS). Public records can also show relevant sales information, but the data is not as detailed or timely.

As you can see in Table 7.1, the four properties are similar in size, condition, and age. Often such comparisons are more complicated, depending on the neighborhoods and property differentiations. But I wanted to provide a simplistic example that highlights the general process and concept behind this valuation method.

The general idea behind the sales comparison approach is to make pricing adjustments to the comparable properties in order to make them more like the subject property. For example, the subject property has two fireplaces, which is

Table 7.1
Sales Comparison Approach

	Subject Property	Comparable No. 1	Comparable No. 2	Comparable No. 3
Age of comparable sales (days)		30	46	92
Site	Average	Average	Average	Average
View	Average	Average	Average	Average
Design and appeal	Average	Average	Average	Average
Quality of construction	Average	Average	Average	Average
Age (years)	20	20	19	22
Fireplace	2	1	0	2
Patio/deck	Yes	Yes	Yes	Yes
Pool	No	No	No	Yes
Sales price		$ 192,000	$ 184,000	$ 215,000
Price adjustments:				
Fireplace		1,500	3,000	
Pool				(10,000)
Adjusted sales price		$ 193,500	$ 187,000	$ 205,000
Living area square footage	1,874	1,754	1,700	1,912
Price per square footage		$ 110.3	$ 110.0	$ 107.2
Average price per square footage	$ 109.2			
Value of subject property	$ 204,601			

a feature that adds value to a property. Comparable No. 1 has only one fireplace, so the appraiser needs to assume that this property has two fireplaces in order to make it more comparable to the subject property. The appraiser assigned a value of $1,500 to a fireplace, so the adjusted sales price of Comparable No. 1 is increased by $1,500 to reflect what the selling price might have been had the property had two fireplaces. The same logic applies to Comparable No. 2. In this case, the appraiser increased the value of this property by $3,000 to show what the house might have been worth had it had two fireplaces instead of none.

Comparable No. 3 has a swimming pool and the subject property does not. Therefore, the appraiser removed the value of the swimming pool (assumed to be $10,000) from the value of Comparable No. 3 in order to make the two properties more comparable. Doing so lowers the adjusted sales price of Comparable No. 3 to reflect the removal of the pool.

After the adjustments are made to the comparable properties, an average price per square foot is computed. By doing so, the appraiser is determining how much each square foot of each home's livable space (usually defined as the combined areas of a house under heating or air conditioning) is worth. Using the information in Table 7.1, the average value per square foot of living area for the three comparable properties is $109.2. Since the subject property contains 1,874 square feet of living area, a value is determined by multiplying $109.2 per square foot by 1,874 square feet. The result is an estimated value of $204,601 for the subject property.

As you can see, even in this simple example where all four properties are so similar, this can be a very subjective analysis. There are many more variables that can be assessed when comparing properties such as lot sizes, site access, and floor plans. The sales comparison approach is most suitable when the same type of property is being exchanged periodically in the market. As you can imagine, this valuation method is usually best applicable when dealing with residential properties because of the generic nature and abundant supply of comparables.

THE COST APPROACH

The cost approach to valuing real estate is based upon summing the costs of land and the costs to construct any existing buildings or improvements. How much would it cost to buy the underlying land and build a similar structure as the one being valued? Once you know the answer to this question, you are almost done with your valuation. However, a brand new property should certainly be worth more than an older property. To address this difference, the values of any buildings or improvements are depreciated and reduced to reflect their ages and any potentially obsolete features.

The example in Table 7.2 illustrates the cost approach to valuing real estate using the same subject property that we valued under the sales comparison approach in Table 7.1. As indicated, the first step under the cost approach is to value the underlying land. Next, the cost to construct the home is estimated at $85 per square foot. Appraisers and industry professionals tend to know the average costs involved in building residential and commercial properties. In addition,

Table 7.2
Cost Approach

Estimated land value	$	35,000
Cost to construct house:		
1,874 square feet at $85 per square foot		159,290
Cost to construct garage:		
400 square feet at $25 per square foot		10,000
Appliances, floor coverings, heating and air systems		15,000
Total estimated costs with new construction	$	219,290
Less: Physical depreciation		(25,000)
Estimated value by cost approach	$	194,290

there are companies such as Marshall & Swift that publish construction cost guidance, which can be used as a reliable source of data.

Since the living area of the house is 1,874 square feet, at $85 per square foot, we derive a cost to construct this home of $159,290. This means that today it would cost this amount to build the same size house. Outside of the living area is the garage. Since this is a more simplistic structure, it is estimated to only cost $25 per square foot to build a garage, which results in another $10,000 of estimated costs. Additional features like floor coverings, appliances, and heating and air conditioning systems add another $15,000 of costs.

The total estimated costs derived in our analysis imply that to purchase a similar parcel of land and build the same size house today would cost approximately $219,290. But this would be a brand new house. Our subject property is 20 years old. To adjust our analysis for the age of the subject property, we assumed that the property has depreciated in value by $25,000. Note that this depreciation was based on physical condition. Additional dollars might be deducted from a property's value based on criteria such as outdated styles, floor plans, and features, thus adding additional subjectivity to the analysis.

Even though all properties can be assessed using the cost approach, older properties are more difficult and are more subjective to evaluate. The older the property, the more subjective becomes the estimation of depreciation for age and functional and economic obsolescence. The cost approach is often the best valuation method when looking at unique properties having a specific use. In addition, this method is often used in conjunction with another method such as the sales comparison approach.

THE INCOME APPROACH

The income approach to valuing real estate is most often used for income-producing commercial properties. There are several ways to value a property using an income approach. One of the most common methods relies on assessing a value based upon a property's level of net operating income (NOI).

In Table 7.3 is an example of the computation of a property's NOI.

Table 7.3
Net Operating Income (NOI) Calculation

	Monthly	Annual
Income		
Gross rent	$ 8,000	$ 96,000
Vacancy factor (10%)	(800)	(9,600)
Net rent	7,200	86,400
Expenses		
Management fees	288	3,456
Maintenance reserve	360	4,320
Utilities	425	5,100
Taxes	720	8,640
Insurance	144	1,728
Other expenses	225	2,700
Total expenses	2,162	25,944
Net operating income	$ 5,038	$ 60,456

Once the expected NOI for one or more years is computed for a property, some valuation technique is employed. The simplest approach uses a net income capitalization rate or "cap rate." Based on an investor's required return on a property and the expected returns from similar properties, a market capitalization rate is chosen.

Under the net income capitalization approach, if an investor requires a return of 9.5% per year on a similar property as the one identified in Table 7.3, he can take the annual NOI of $60,456 and divide this number by 9.5%. This would imply that the property is worth approximately $636,379.

The net income capitalization approach is best used when a property's cash flows are expected to remain fairly constant for the near and mid-future. This method is also best used for smaller properties having a limited number of leases.

A simpler, but often less reliable method under the income approach is based upon using a gross rent multiplier to derive an estimate of a property's value. Assume a property similar to the one identified in Table 7.3 recently sold for $800,000 and its annual rental income was $125,000. This would imply a gross rent multiplier of 6.4 ($800,000 sales price divided by $125,000 of annual rent). To assist in assessing the value of our property, we would take $96,000 of annual rent from Table 7.3 and multiply this number by 6.4, which would result in an approximate value of $614,400.

Gross rent multipliers often serve as a sanity check and are usually not used in isolation. When looking at many properties, using a gross rent multiplier can help to weed out overpriced properties and allow an investor to focus on more realistically priced potential investments. Looking at a property's value using multiple valuation techniques is always a good idea and can provide investors with greater comfort.

Before we talk about the most complicated method under the income approach that is most often used for valuing larger and more complicated properties and projects having varying levels of cash flow from period to period, we must first talk about the time value of money.

THE TIME VALUE OF MONEY

If someone were to offer you $100 today or $100 a year from now, which would you take? I would take the $100 today for two reasons. First, having the money now eliminates any risk that I might not be paid in one year. Second, I can take the $100 today, invest it, and hopefully have more than $100 in one year. Let us say that I purchase a one-year certificate of deposit from a bank that pays 5% annual interest. In one year when the CD matures, I should have $105. Likewise, if I had to pay someone $100, it would behoove me to pay in a year rather than now, were it an option. This is the essence of the time value of money.

In the example just mentioned, the future value of $100 one year from today, assuming a 5% interest rate, is $105. Conversely, assuming the same 5% interest rate, the value today (the "present value") of $105 to be received in one year is $100. Therefore, if someone offers you the choice of receiving $100 today or $100 a year from now and you feel that you should earn 5% on a one-year loan to this person, then the $100 payable in one year is really only worth $95.24 today. I backed into this number by using a simple formula: $100/1.05 = $95.24. It can be tested by multiplying $95.24 by 1.05 (1 plus the assumed interest rate) to get back to $100.

The time value of money applies to all forms of investing and real estate is no exception. The basic principle is based upon the fact that the sooner investors receive cash flow, the greater their return on an investment. In addition, when expenses and other cash outflows can be delayed, doing so can also greatly enhance an investor's return. Let us review the principles of a *discounted cash flow analysis* to further solidify these points.

A discounted cash flow analysis is another valuation method that falls under the income approach and it is based upon the time value of money. A discounted cash flow analysis is a much more complicated methodology when compared to using a calculation based on NOI or gross rent. This method is often used for larger and more expensive properties such as shopping centers and office buildings.

The rationale behind a discounted cash flow analysis is that a project is going to have cash inflows and cash outflows and these net cash amounts have value. Based upon an investor's targeted rate of return for a specific project, future expected cash flows are valued or "discounted" into today's dollars. Let us look at Table 7.4 to better understand this concept.

As can be seen in Table 7.4, the cash flows for the property identified in Table 7.3 have been extended and forecasted for a five-year period. The time period used for a discounted cash flow analysis is usually no greater than 10 years. The longer the time frame used, the harder it becomes to forecast future cash flows and the less certain these assumptions become. If an investor is valuing a project with a shorter expected duration, then a lower number of years would be used.

Table 7.4
Discounted Cash Flow Analysis

	Year 1	Year 2	Year 3	Year 4	Year 5
Income					
Gross rent	$ 96,000	$ 98,880	$ 101,846	$ 104,902	$ 108,049
Vacancy factor (10%)	(9,600)	(9,888)	(10,185)	(10,490)	(10,805)
Net rent	86,400	88,992	91,661	94,412	97,244
Expenses					
Management fees	3,456	3,560	3,666	3,776	3,890
Maintenance reserve	4,320	4,450	4,583	4,721	4,862
Utilities	5,100	5,151	5,203	5,255	5,307
Taxes	8,640	8,726	8,814	8,902	8,991
Insurance	1,728	1,745	1,763	1,780	1,798
Other expenses	2,700	2,727	2,754	2,782	2,810
Total expenses	25,944	26,359	26,783	27,216	27,658
Net sales price of property					725,000
Net cash flow	$ 60,456	$ 62,633	$ 64,878	$ 67,196	$ 794,586
Net present value—10% discount rate					$694,738.81
Net present value—15% discount rate					$576,058.42
Net present value—20% discount rate					$483,152.82
Net present value—25% discount rate					$409,561.55

For example, if you are investing in a construction project that is expected to take two years to complete before selling the land and building, then two years of cash flows would be used to represent the life of the project. To be thorough and conservative with your valuation, you might assume in one or more scenarios that the project gets delayed and therefore use a longer period of time (i.e., three years) for your analysis.

Typically, a discounted cash flow analysis will assume debt financing to enhance profitability. Table 7.4 excluded this assumption in order to keep the analysis simple. However, a key difference between NOI and the net cash flows used in a discounted cash flow analysis is that interest and principal payments associated with any debt financing are excluded from NOI while included as cash outflows in net cash flow calculations.

In Table 7.4, we are attempting to back into a value for the subject property based upon the expected future cash flows and our desired annual return. Our targeted annual return is represented by the "discount rate" used to reduce and convert future expected cash flows into today's dollars. For example, if we believe that an annual return of 15% should be earned by buying and owning this property for five years, then we would be willing to pay approximately $576,058. At this price, assuming that all of our assumptions and the resulting cash flows were accurate over the next five years, we would earn a return of approximately 15% per year for each of the five years.

In Table 7.4, we assume the subject property can be sold in five years and generate net cash flow after selling costs of $725,000. This is a best guess at an event that may or may not take place in the future. In addition, assumed rent and operating costs may be more or less than expected. The longer the forecast, the more uncertainty involved.

There are many variations of how a discounted cash flow analysis can be performed, but our example covers the general principles. You can buy software to perform these calculations. Such programs allow users to enter assumptions and generate results. I used a simple "net present value" formula in Microsoft Excel for the example in Table 7.4. There is a free model on my Web site that uses these same principles to compute estimated annual returns when buying single-family homes for investment that will be described further in a later chapter.

It is important that investors understand the principles of a discounted cash flow analysis and the time value of money before attempting to perform their own analysis. This is one of the complexities associated with commercial real estate investing. Also, when unrealistic assumptions are used, the results of the analysis will be misleading.

SUMMARY

Appraisers may use all three approaches or any combination of the approaches above to determine a specific property's value. Depending upon the type of property, one or more approaches may be clearly more applicable. For example, residential housing values are most often appraised using the comparable sales approach. Unique properties with few or no comparables are often valued using the cost approach. Income-producing commercial properties are usually valued based upon some type of income approach. The larger and more complex the property, the more complicated the calculation. A small property with one tenant can usually be valued based upon a certain cap rate and one year of NOI. A large commercial shopping center with many tenants may warrant a 10-year discounted cash flow analysis.

Valuation opinions can vary dramatically. I recently witnessed two different appraisers value the same property at $8 million and $24 million within a six-month period. While this example is extreme, investors need to derive their own conclusions when it comes to the value of a specific property.

As you can see, there are varying levels of subjectivity involved when valuing real estate. This is a primary reason why so many inefficiencies and opportunities exist in real estate investing. Since there is no liquid or standardized trading market to objectively assess and value real estate transactions, substantial variations in value can result for the same property. In addition, each property is unique. Different property features, conditions, ages, locations, etc. all result in differing values.

We will talk more about assessing a proper rate of return and determining when properties are under and overpriced. For now, just realize that there are several universal methods to valuing real estate and that most values are determined by appraisers and investors using one or more of the general approaches referenced in this chapter.

Chapter 8

NEGOTIATING THE BEST PRICE AND TERMS

Real estate markets are both illiquid and inefficient. Transactions take time to materialize and sales contracts may often terminate due to various contingencies. In addition, the specific terms of many real estate transactions are not available to other investors. While these attributes can cause frustration and lead to panic for the wrong investor in the wrong market, they can also result in favorable investment opportunities for savvy and experienced investors.

The ability to negotiate the best pricing and terms for property acquisitions is a rare skill that is enhanced with experience. Often this entails learning some lessons the hard way. Obtaining your ultimate goals and striking what at least appears to be a win-win transaction for you and your counterpart should be your targeted end result. Allowing ego to participate in a negotiation and focusing solely upon winning at the expense of someone else is not a productive mentality.

When buying and selling residential properties, your counterparts are often less experienced and more emotional than when transacting with commercial properties. But human emotion tends to get the best of all of us at one time or another. Maintaining focus and a cool head is essential when it comes to the more challenging negotiations.

I have seen negotiations swing back and forth for millions of dollars. Sometimes it seems like an agreement will never be reached, but then someone budges on a deal breaking point and the negotiations begin again. Other times deals that are almost certain to close are abruptly terminated and never resurrected.

There are many reasons why some transactions never get done, but usually there is a disagreement between parties or maybe just an irrational perspective by one person. Maybe a seller is maintaining an unrealistic price target. Perhaps zoning, environmental, or flooding problems are discovered. Maybe the seller cannot provide clean title to a property. The list goes on. But even after all the surprises have been uncovered, there are usually terms and a price that will result in the sale of any property.

A good negotiator is resourceful and creative and continues to attack problems and obstacles from many angles. Below are qualities that I have witnessed in some of the better and more successful real estate investors.

LEAVE YOUR EGO AT THE DOOR

It is human nature to bring a certain level of emotion and ego into the decision-making process. Some of the best business people that I have ever met are able to set aside their personal feelings in order to make the best business decisions. In essence, they follow the "business is business" philosophy. Clearly, this is easier said than done and I often find myself struggling with this concept. It is difficult to not let people annoy you during a negotiation. This is because your goals and perspectives usually differ from those of the person you are negotiating with. A better deal for you is usually a worse deal for him and vice versa. Of course, there will be conflict and disagreement.

When my ego and personality seem to be getting the best of me and affecting my business decisions, I consciously try to stop myself and focus solely on the best outcome under the circumstances. Sometimes this means giving up something to the other side no matter how ridiculous or unfair it seems to me. Other times, it means walking away from a deal. But my key objective is to leave my ego out of the process.

I can remember dealing with sellers and buyers of our rental properties and how upset my wife would become over the negotiation process. Admittedly, I had my moments as well. But I tried to objectively see the most favorable outcome for each transaction, which often meant swallowing my pride and making the best deal that I could. My suggestion to you is to fight your natural urges of taking things personal. "Business is business" and the decisions made by the better business people are not based on spite, revenge, egotism, or pride.

PLAN AHEAD AND STRATEGIZE

The better negotiators plan ahead and strategize about their objectives and about what they are willing to give up for something in return. When acting as potential buyers, these people know what a property is worth before they say a word to a Realtor or seller. They know what they are willing to pay and what they would like to pay. They overly stress the negative and under stress and counterargue the positive aspects of a property.

When selling properties, strong negotiators spend considerable time deriving a proper asking price. They consider the most favorable attributes of their properties that add value and that can be referenced to potential buyers during negotiations. They overly stress the positive and under stress and counterargue the negative aspects of a property.

Responses to any offers and counteroffers made or received are carefully contemplated before any type of answer is provided. A good negotiator considers the positions and objectives of the people with which he is negotiating. What is important to them? What is their particular circumstance? What factors can I use to my advantage?

People that walk blindly into a negotiation without contemplating their position or the positions of their opponents are unprepared and often severely disadvantaged. Why does this person want to buy or sell this property? What does he intend to do with the property or sales proceeds? How badly does he need or want the money or the property?

If I own the one remaining piece of land that is surrounded by other parcels owned by the same developer, I have bargaining power that should warrant a premium sales price. If a seller of a property does not need the money, perhaps he would be willing to provide seller financing, which would reduce my cash investment. This could increase my return on invested capital and I might be able to meet a seller's price in return for such a trade-off. Maybe a seller wants to sell his property now, but he needs to occupy the property for some period before I take possession. Perhaps he would take a lower price in return for a six-month lease.

Creativity is an important tool for the successful negotiator. Negotiating real estate pricing and terms is not a rigid, black and white, robotic function. There is more to it than offering a price, receiving a counteroffer, submitting another counteroffer, etc. until a deal is reached or terminated. Plan ahead, know as much as you can about the property and the surrounding circumstances of the seller or buyer, think out of the box, and be willing to pursue your objectives from multiple angles.

KEEP YOUR INTENTIONS TO YOUR SELF

Consider sellers of personal residences. Situations including divorce, recent or pending moves, and unemployment can all lead to a weakened negotiating stance when buyers are aware of these factors. Long marketing periods can also imply desperation. Regardless of a seller's motivation for selling, the longer his property sits on the market, the greater the delay he has in manifesting his post-sale intentions.

I often find residential Realtors to be their client's worst enemy. They are equally or even more motivated to see you buy or sell a property. I have seen Realtors befriend individuals and other Realtors on the opposing side of transactions in an attempt to close deals and earn their commissions. I have had Realtors representing sellers tell me that their clients were extremely desperate and motivated and that I should just make any offer. Armed with this information, you can bet my offers were really low!

As numerous buyers and sellers filled the residential housing markets in the early to mid-2000s, after passing a simple state exam, countless inexperienced Realtors entered the market searching for fortune. Just like stockbrokers often recommend those investments to their clients that pay them the highest commissions, Realtors can also be bought. Take this as a warning—do not trust your Realtor and divulge only the information that you want communicated to the people that you are transacting with.

Just like in the Godfather movies, successful real estate negotiators keep their emotions and thoughts to themselves (or within the family!). Just make sure that you can completely trust anyone involved in a potential transaction before you share your intentions.

CONSIDER HOW YOU COMMUNICATE

People can be more or less receptive to an offer or counteroffer based upon the tone and mode of communication in which it is made. For example, aggressive and offensive conversations and forms of written correspondence can produce unpleasant and unproductive responses from recipients based upon their interpretations and personalities. Remember, human emotion is hard to contain and no one wants to feel abused or manipulated.

When someone sends me a contract with bold strikes and insistent and demanding comments, I instantly do not like them. In doing so, they are trying to bully me and take control of the negotiation. I would much rather receive an offer that reflects thought and consideration accompanied by a pleasant and professional cover letter. Even lowball bids that are well below an offering price are often better received when presented in a cordial manner.

Particularly when buying and selling residential properties, but also applicable for commercial properties, I find that explaining why I feel a particular property is worth a certain value can be helpful to my counterpart. For example, when buying residential properties, I would often send a cover letter or e-mail with an offer or counteroffer explaining the supporting rationale behind the price that I was willing to pay or accept.

I might tell a homeowner that while he has a beautiful home, as an investor my decisions are based purely on numerical calculations. In addition, I might list some of the key costs that would be required to preserve the home's value. Examples might include an aged roof and air conditioning and heating system, new carpeting and paint. Then I might acknowledge that another buyer seeking a personal residence might be willing to pay more, but based upon my calculations, I either need a substantial repair allowance or a much lower sales price in order to meet my minimum return requirements. At this point, I may end the conversation or correspondence by telling the seller that I need to move on to the next property and thank him for his time and sincerely wish him good luck on a quick and prosperous sale.

In the example above, I might be bargain hunting and my minimum annual expected return might be 15–20%, but that does not mean that I need to insult anyone. Chances are that my bids will get turned down on numerous properties based on such a high profitability threshold, but sellers want to sell and the chances are good that under the right circumstance one or more of my offers will be accepted.

If I came into a person's home or sent any form of correspondence stating that the house was run down and worth substantially less than he thinks, this would be an unnecessary source of contention. Ego may immediately kick in, and the seller might rightly get offended. This is not a productive way of starting a negotiation and attempting to reach your goal.

THE WIN-WIN APPROACH

When negotiating any type of transaction, each party wants to feel as though they have won. At the very least, no one wants to feel taken advantage of or manipulated. Rather than approach a negotiation with high ego and the goal of winning at the other party's expense, a more productive strategy is to focus on achieving your objectives while attempting to meet the needs of your counterpart as well.

People tend to be more willing to give when they do not feel threatened, annoyed, or insulted. Again, this is just basic human behavior. Often times, your objectives are not very different from your counterpart's. This may seem counterintuitive assuming that purchase price is the only important factor. He wants to pay the lowest price or receive the highest price and you want just the opposite. But this is a black and white perspective. People that enter a negotiation this way are being narrow minded and, in most cases, will not reach the most optimal outcome.

As mentioned above, knowing as much as possible about a counterpart can be a key negotiating tool. Maybe a seller has a low cost basis in a property and the sale is going to generate a large tax liability. Perhaps this tax expense could be spread out over many years if the seller agrees to provide a portion of the financing. Maybe a seller would be looking to reinvest cash into your project, thus reducing the amount of equity capital needed.

When preparing for a negotiation, always ask for more than you expect to receive. A simple example would be to always ask for a higher sales price or a lower purchase price than you feel is reasonable. But keep going. If a counterpart wants a later closing date, ask for an earlier one. If she wants an earlier closing date, ask for a later one. Request that the buyer or seller pay all closing costs. Ask for a larger repair allowance or that all defects and maintenance items referenced in a home inspection be corrected no matter how immaterial.

One might think that asking so much might be overreaching and lead to further distance between buyer and seller. I do not disagree. However, the more differences between parties, the more points that can be conceded in exchange for others. The more items you give in on, the more your counterpart believes he has won. Even if it appears that you are giving in on two issues for every one that he allows, you are still getting closer to your objective. Some people would allow their egos to dominate under this strategy even though they are conceding on unwanted or expected issues in order to get closer to their ultimate goal. A strong negotiator is not concerned with his counterpart's opinion and is only focused on his true objectives.

In addition to creating what at least appears to be a win-win scenario, you may be surprised and be granted some of the things that you thought were unreasonable. Maybe your counterpart agrees to pay 75% of all closing costs. Maybe he fixes every repair item no matter how insignificant. You never know until you ask.

Also remember that the more you ask for, the more room you have to negotiate. If a seller wants $200,000 for a property and you offer $170,000, there is little room to negotiate between counteroffers. Maybe you end up splitting the difference and agree on $185,000. But if you offer $150,000, there is a greater chance that you will pay something less.

Many people feel intimidated when making low offers (and even when setting high asking prices) or requesting certain provisions and terms. There is a fine line between an offer that will at least generate a counteroffer and one that will just be dismissed. But your chances of appearing sincere and being taken seriously will be increased based upon the teachings within this chapter. So stand your ground, fight any intimidation, and do not take rejection personally. When dealing with such an illiquid asset class, you will be surprised how badly many sellers want to believe that a sale is possible. In addition, in favorable real estate markets when limited opportunities exist, many buyers will also be willing to pay substantially more than you might think.

BE CAREFUL OF THE WORDS "YES" AND "NO"

Saying "yes" to a seller or buyer's first offer will usually result in you paying a higher purchase price or receiving a lower sales price. People at all levels of negotiating skill are expecting at least one counteroffer. When you immediately agree to a seller's asking price or to a buyer's offering price, you have left money on the table. If your counterpart is one of the rare exceptions and is nonresponsive to a counteroffer, chances are you will still have the ability to accept the original offer.

With quick acceptance and without a counteroffer, your counterparty immediately assumes that he could have done better and begins to question what he is getting or giving up. This is especially true when you immediately accept an offer that is too low. This can cause second guessing and raise doubt. Maybe there is something wrong with the property. Maybe I am paying too much. Thoughts like this on the opposing side can increase the chances of a deal collapsing.

Always maintain respect and sincerity with your counterpart no matter how much you disagree. You can always end your current negotiation session by telling him to please contact you if he changes his mind. You might be surprised by how many times someone regrets letting a buyer or seller slip away. And when someone calls you later with a change of heart, your negotiating position often grows stronger.

When a counterparty says "no," do not necessarily perceive this as the end of your negotiations. Sometimes this may be ego taking over and a small concession can get things restarted. Other times, the counterparty or his Realtor might call you and start the process again (assuming you left the door open for such discussions). Sometimes, when I see a property on the market for a significant period after a stalled negotiation, I send a quick e-mail to the seller or his Realtor and re-extend my offer. Since I was the one to reestablish contact, this allows the seller to still maintain his pride, while restoring the possibility of selling his property. I may still seek the same deal or an even better deal, but in exchange for a minor concession or two, sometimes an agreement can still be reached.

When you say "no" you limit any future negotiations. Often it is better to leave yourself more options. The phrase "take it or leave it" can help or harm your negotiation. On one hand, it is sometimes good to show flexibility. For example, if you are making an extremely low offer, you probably want to imply some flexibility in the price you are willing to pay. On the other hand, "take it or leave it" can be a strong ending negotiation tactic to force a counterpart's hand. Just be ready to walk if his response is unfavorable.

SUMMARY

The difference between a good and a bad negotiator can equate to thousands or even millions of dollars. The key to successfully negotiating is to initially and continually strategize. When seeking to buy real estate, do not just go from property to property shooting from the hip and generating offers as you go. When selling property, carefully consider the right asking price. In addition, think about and plan a proper response to every offer and counteroffer. Restrict your ego from intervening and learn how to stroke the egos of others in order to achieve your end objectives.

There are numerous books, seminars, and other forums on the subject of negotiation and readers can benefit from such teachings. But the best negotiators have learned through practice. Having the right personality can clearly provide an advantage. Facing confrontation and being accepting of rejection can be favorable character traits. In addition, having the ability to convince people to act (i.e., the salesperson) can also be a great asset.

Anyone can become a good negotiator. Depending on the circumstance, this can be done directly or through a Realtor. I find that many Realtors tend to distort my messages or dominate my intentions with their own underlying objectives. But clearly some are better than others and many are quite skilled at the negotiation process. Discussing strategy with someone you trust can be beneficial and shed new light and perspectives on a situation. How you communicate verbally and in writing is another aspect. The key is to use the method in which you are most comfortable and most powerful so that your ultimate message can be best conveyed.

Chapter 9

FINDING THE RIGHT LENDER

As mentioned earlier, the use of leverage can greatly enhance the profitability of an investment and better an investor's ability to compete with other bidders when attempting to purchase a property. While there are many factors that affect the general values of real estate, generous financing terms and low interest rates often lead to higher property values.

Just as real estate markets move in cycles, so do the lending terms offered by banks and other financial institutions. For example, it is now widely known that during the residential housing market bonanza that took place during the early and mid-2000s, lenders were extremely competitive and aggressive when financing single-family homes. In fact, lenders were so eager to lend money that, in many cases, they neglected to verify borrower income or request proper documentation. Lenders fought to outbid one another with low interest rates, quick approvals, and loose lending standards.

Not only were borrowers receiving unprecedented terms for loans secured by residential housing, investors within other sectors of the real estate markets were also getting great deals. Developers seeking to buy land to construct and sell houses at historically high prices were receiving high loan-to-value ratios, while avoiding the need for supporting income and personal guarantees. Everyone just assumed that property values would keep rising even as housing became increasingly unaffordable for more and more people.

As the housing markets began to weaken and turn downward, lenders (and their regulators) began to realize that lending policies had been imprudent and unsustainable. In fact, the dramatic rise in residential loan delinquencies and foreclosures has caused lenders to take hundreds of billions of dollars of losses and has played a key role in throwing the entire economy into recession.

As aggressive financing terms were overly available in the booming residential markets, loan terms on properties being used or intended to be used for commercial purposes (i.e., retail shopping, restaurants, office buildings, etc.) were becoming more and more aggressive as well. While commercial markets have not experienced nearly as significant a disruption, property values have begun to decline and financing has become more expensive and much less abundant. It appears that many commercial real estate markets have peaked and that further reductions in value and higher borrower default rates are on the horizon.

Now that many lenders have and continue to experience the financial pain and embarrassment associated with their aggressive lending practices, the overall lending cycle has shifted from one extreme to the other. Many buyers no longer qualify for financing. Within such an environment, even borrowers with strong credit often have difficulty receiving lender approval and such approval can take a considerable amount of time and require substantial documentation. This is something that investors need to consider. When markets turn ugly, there may be countless buying opportunities. However, available financing may become very limited and the terms much more conservative.

The intent of this chapter is to highlight various sources of borrower capital and identify the most important terms and features to consider.

DEBT VERSUS EQUITY

If you are going to be an ongoing investor in real estate, your contacts and relationships with lenders and other capital providers will be key assets. Depending on the complexity and perceived risk of a particular deal, randomly calling upon lenders and investors can often result in limited success. Knowing someone that trusts you and believes in the viability of your investment choices can go a long way. Such a person can help you to obtain and expedite approvals and lead to better terms and interest rates.

Quickly receiving financing commitments and having the ability to close transactions fast is a great resource. Having committed capital from a reliable source can be attractive to a seller and enhance your negotiating position. Sellers are much more likely to make price concessions when dealing with buyers having preapproved financing and the ability to purchase their properties within a few weeks.

Finding debt financing (i.e., bank and other types of loans) is usually easier than finding someone to invest with you as an equity partner. Equity is subordinate to debt and lenders want to see some type of equity investment before making a loan. This is because when a borrower can no longer make his loan payments and a lender must foreclose and take possession of the underlying property, any equity investment made by the borrower aids in preserving the lender's collateral position.

Equity serves as protection against losses for lenders. For example, if you buy a property for $100 and a lender provides a loan for $80 to facilitate the purchase, you will need to invest $20 of equity. If you default on your loan, the lender only needs to sell the property for $80 to be repaid in full. The $20 equity investment serves as a cushion for the lender in case a property declines in value or has to be sold quickly.

TRADITIONAL FINANCING FOR SINGLE-FAMILY HOMES

When seeking financing for residential property investments, lenders should be abundant. This is not to say that you will be approved for financing, but you should be able to find a variety of independent mortgage brokers in town and numerous lending representatives within your local bank offices. A mortgage broker is an individual or company that earns a fee for bringing borrowers and lenders together. Mortgage brokers have relationships with numerous lenders and can often find the best terms and interest rates on behalf of a borrower.

I have always found that obtaining two to four quotes in order to get the best interest rate and other financing terms is very worthwhile. In addition, some lenders (although a much smaller number) are sometimes willing to provide higher loan-to-value limits beyond the normal 80%. I often find that mortgage brokers (as opposed to traditional banks) are best at finding these specific lenders.

While I believe that investors should always seek multiple quotes, there can clearly be value in developing a relationship with one or more mortgage brokers and bank loan officers. A loan officer is a representative of a bank or other financial institution that serves as a borrower's point of contact and gathers documents, orders appraisals, and seeks ultimate approval for your loan.

Years ago when my wife and I were buying single-family properties, I had a relationship with a local loan officer from one of the larger national banks. Not only did I finance and refinance numerous residential properties with this person, I also referred many of my friends and colleagues that were seeking to buy or refinance houses for personal use or investment.

My relationship with this lender allowed me to get the best interest rates without having to extensively negotiate (although I always requested at least one other quote from a competitor just to keep him honest). In addition, I was able to get current interest rate quotes on weekends when bidding for houses. This loan officer was also familiar with all of my financial information and would "lock" my interest rate as soon as a contract was being signed so that I knew exactly what my mortgage payment would be before buying the house. He was also willing to provide a letter immediately upon my request stating that I was preapproved for financing and that he could commit to closing in three to four weeks. This showed sellers that I had the ability to close a transaction and do so quickly.

TRADITIONAL FINANCING FOR COMMERCIAL PROPERTIES

The most attractive and appropriate sources to seek financing for commercial properties often depend upon the specific type of project or property. Each sector of real estate will generally be viewed as more or less risky by potential lenders. This perception is often magnified during specific real estate markets or sector cycles. For example, properties used or intended to be used as restaurants or gas stations are usually viewed as being unfavorable collateral for a lender since so many of these business operations fail. However, hotels and office buildings can become more or less out of favor for lenders depending upon recent specific sector performance. If the financial and real estate news is constantly stating that office vacancy rates are high and increasing and that these types of properties are overvalued, then lenders will tend to avoid them.

When lenders take substantial losses due to defaulting loans in a specific real estate sector, they tend to avoid additional loans to the same sector regardless of how favorable the credit strength of a borrower and the underlying property. Banks and other financial institutions can often overreact to bad news. For example, recently many lenders have taken large losses on loans to home builders and those backed by land investments. Now many lenders, including some of the largest banks in the country, are unwilling to even consider providing loans collateralized by land under any circumstance. Years down the road when land is back in favor, the same lenders will most likely be eager to provide such financing.

Your chances are much better when seeking a loan on a real estate investment that is within a sector that is performing well. But often the best buying opportunities include out-of-favor real estate sectors and properties. When markets turn downward, lenders can find such properties even less desirable. The number of willing buyers and lenders can decline dramatically. In such cases, investors may need to work harder and more creatively to obtain financing and be willing to invest more of their own cash. Such factors need to be considered when projecting an investment's expected profitability.

The size of a commercial loan can also determine the most appropriate source of potential financing. Loans up to $10 million might be handled locally by a commercial bank. I have found that this number can vary depending upon the size of a particular city. Smaller cities often have smaller lending limits.

Larger loans may need to be "syndicated," meaning that several lenders participate and each one funds a portion of the total loan amount. For example, if you need a $20 million loan, perhaps one bank will fund $10 million and two others will fund $5 million each. From your perspective, the process can be quite seamless. You will make your monthly payments to one lender referred to as the "agent" or "lead" bank. This is usually the financial institution that arranged the total financing package and marketed it to the participating lenders.

Depending upon the perceived risk associated with your loan, the lead lender might be willing to advance the entire amount and then sell portions to other lenders after the loan has been closed. In this case, you may never know that part of your loan is owned by one or more other banks. In other cases, the lead lender may be unwilling to assume the entire risk of your loan and therefore require that other banks be found before committing to fund the loan.

Wall Street investment firms can be another source of commercial real estate financing. Usually a loan will need to be at least $5 million before capturing the attention of such firms, but the terms can be very favorable. Often commercial loans that are originated or purchased by an investment bank are securitized. Securitization entails the aggregation of a pool of loans and then the marketing and sale of bonds collateralized by such loans to investors.

Let us use a simple example to illustrate the general mechanics of a securitization. Assume that you and some colleagues borrow $10 million from a Wall Street investment bank. Your loan officer might be in a local branch of this firm, but the securitization would most likely be done out of the bank's headquarters or a division specializing in capital markets and the sale of securities.

Assume that the investment bank that loaned you $10 million made $1 billion in loans to 50 investors. This means that the average loan amount is about $20 million. In order for the bank to recycle its capital and have the ability to make more loans, it needs to sell its existing loans or sell bonds collateralized by the loans (a securitization).

Using a simplistic securitization structure, assume that the investment bank aggregates its $1 billion of loans and sells bonds backed by the principal and interest payments scheduled to be received on the loans. For example, $100 million of three-year bonds, $200 million of five-year bonds, $200 million of seven-year bonds, and $525 million of ten-year bonds might be sold to investors (notice that there is a $25 million profit). As the monthly principal and interest payments are paid by borrowers on the $1 billion of commercial loans, these payments are passed on to bondholders.

By executing a securitization, the investment bank was able to sell enough bonds to recover the $1 billion that it had lent to borrowers plus a $25 million profit. Now the bank can make another $1 billion worth of loans to customers and start the entire process again. As a borrower, you will continue to make your monthly loan payments to the same bank and be unaware of the fact that your loan serves as collateral for part of a $1 billion securitization.

While the example provided assumes the securitization of commercial loans, the same process takes place with most residential loans. If you have a loan on your home, the chances are great that it has been securitized and your payments are being used to repay bondholders.

Large institutional lenders can be great sources of financing for larger projects. Insurance companies, pension funds, hedge funds, and mortgage REITs all manage large sums of money that needs to be invested. Providing loans to real estate investors can be an attractive and profitable option for these entities.

Lenders normally favor lending money on commercial real estate that produces income. This is because income-producing real estate generates cash flow that can be used to make interest payments and to repay loans. This cash flow comes from the tenants that pay rent to occupy the commercial properties, such as when a supermarket rents space in a shopping center or a corporation rents offices. But many real estate projects do not produce any income and might not be expected to for some time. Obtaining financing for these projects can be much more difficult.

An acquisition and development loan, or "A&D loan," is used for the acquisition of property and its ultimate development. For example, the site of every residential and commercial building was at one point vacant land. Builders need financing to buy land, obtain the necessary permits and zoning, perform grading, and add infrastructure items such as sewer, power, water, and sidewalks. They then need money to build the intended structures (i.e., a residential community or commercial shopping center).

A&D loans are usually made by local banks and specialty lenders familiar with the particular geographic areas where the underlying properties are located. For large multimillion dollar projects, institutional lenders and Wall Street investment banks might provide financing.

An A&D loan usually carries a higher rate of interest than a loan on income-producing commercial property to compensate lenders for the higher risk. A&D loans are usually repaid from the sale of property or from the proceeds from new and cheaper financing. Once a project reaches a certain development phase, additional lenders are often willing to provide financing. For example, many banks will not lend money to borrowers for the purchase of raw land due to the high perceived risk of such ventures. However, once the land has been properly zoned, construction is ready to begin, and buyers of the ultimate project begin to materialize, the more conservative lenders will begin to show interest.

A borrower might be required to pay a high rate of interest for a two-year loan used to acquire raw land (i.e., 12%) and obtain the necessary political approvals and add the needed infrastructure. Once the project is ready to begin the construction stage, the investor may be able to obtain cheaper construction financing (i.e., a two-year loan at 8%). Upon completion of the project, if the investor chooses to lease the building to a corporate tenant, he might obtain longer term financing at an even lower interest rate (i.e., a ten-year loan at 6.5%).

PREPARING A PROPER LOAN REQUEST PACKAGE

Lenders want to lend to borrowers that have experience and that present themselves in a professional fashion. Be assured that no one will lend you $50 million to build an amusement park when you have no experience or successful track record with construction projects or with running an amusement park. You also will not find financing for a 40-story condominium tower when your biggest project to date has been the construction of a single-tenant property.

For many investors that really want to become experienced in real estate investing, a logical progression might include the ownership and management of a portfolio of single-family homes, perhaps followed by multifamily property (i.e., duplexes and small apartment buildings) and even small commercial property ownership. The investor may limit his investment activities to this universe of investments and do exceptionally well. For someone seeking larger deals, he may begin pooling capital to purchase larger properties.

Finding financing for a single-family residence that you intend to hold as a rental property should be a fairly simple process when compared to obtaining financing for more complex commercial properties. Banks and other lenders will want to see a combination of strong borrower credit and a property that warrants a loan. There will be loan applications and borrower documentation that must be provided (i.e., tax returns, proof of income, etc.). Since lenders handle numerous applications for such financings, the documents and procedures are pretty generic. If you follow the application steps, the process should be fairly straightforward. Any questions can be directed to your mortgage broker or loan officer.

When requesting money for commercial real estate investing, lenders expect a successful track record and a proven ability to manage and own comparable types of properties. The complexity of the particular property you are trying to finance and the type of lender and any prior relationship you have established will dictate the amount of information needed. However, the following are some suggestions when preparing information for a commercial loan request:

- Lenders are impressed when provided relevant information without having to ask. Consider creating a professional packet using a three-ring binder or other bound format. Use a table of contents and multiple tabs identifying each section of material.
- Plan to provide a professional resume showing a progression of key accomplishments. This should be well written with a sensible flow of information. Ensure that there are no misspellings and use a professional format. Irrelevant information can be excluded. For example, no one needs to be alerted to the fact that you bagged groceries during the summer of your junior year of high school. Put yourself in a lender's position when creating your resume. Think about what they would want to see (and what they would not want to see).
- Include resumes for any team members. Your expertise may be limited in one or more areas, but your partner's experience may make up for such limitations. In addition, provide a descriptive overview of any third parties being used for a particular project such as legal and accounting firms.
- A brief written summary (i.e., a page or two) highlighting the merits of the property, why you believe that this is a good investment, and your intentions for the property (i.e., buy and hold, increase tenant occupancy, facilitate new construction or renovation, etc.) should be provided.
- Include any relevant information on the property such as the location, age, permitted uses under any existing zoning, current condition and use, and expected purchase price. If this is an income-producing property, provide information such as the percentage of the property currently leased, the amount of any monthly income, the types of tenants, and the remaining duration of any leases.
- Prepare financial projections showing the expected costs, revenues, and ultimate profits from the property for which you are seeking financing. Included should be the required principal and interest payments on the debt that you are hoping to receive. I recommend including a low interest rate and favorable financing terms in the projections as part of your negotiations strategy. If a lender sees financial projections that assume the receipt of a loan with an 8% interest rate when it would consider lending to you at 7%, chances are that the lender's offered rate will be closer to 8%. However, do not assume an unrealistically low interest rate or you could lose credibility. Financial projections should be neat, well formatted, and easy to read. Usually financial projections are presented by month or quarter for a period of five years or less.
- Include at least two years of tax returns and current financial statements (at least an income statement and balance sheet) for the borrower and any loan guarantors. A local accountant can prepare these if you are unable to do so.
- Provide recent bank and any brokerage account statements showing any material cash balances and other liquid assets.

While the list above is not all inclusive, proactively providing a potential lender with this information will be a great start toward proving your professionalism and justifying your loan request.

KEY FINANCING TERMS

As stated earlier, investors need to have the willingness and the ability to maintain holding power. The willingness is based mostly upon a state of mind, while the ability to hold property through distressed times is often based on having proper financing.

The terms associated with residential financing are usually pretty straightforward since so many of these loans are securitized based on generic documentation. However, depending on the lender and how creative you choose to get with your financing (i.e., higher loan-to-value ratios, etc.), residential loan terms can vary. Ask your mortgage broker or loan officer to confirm the terms you are expecting before choosing a lender and always read any document before signing.

When dealing with commercial financing, the terms can vary significantly by specific transaction. This is especially true when lenders are intending to hold loans versus selling or securitizing them. If your real estate investments become larger and more complex, you will definitely want a real estate attorney to review the loan documents and advise you. Most lenders will want any tenant leases to serve as additional collateral and require documents that subordinate the leases to their loan position. In addition, they will focus more on the value of the underlying real estate to ensure that their collateral is sufficient and secure. Depending on the type of property, lenders may require third-party studies that cover any environmental and flood risks.

When considering and negotiating real estate financing, specific terms may arise based on a particular lender and the type of property being financed. As mentioned, you should read every word of every document before committing even if you have hired an attorney. There have been countless times when my attorneys have ignored certain lender requirements that I raised as potential deal breakers. Remember, most lawyers are reviewing documents to protect you from a legal perspective and not always from a business perspective. It is your job to read and understand these potential issues.

While not all-inclusive and not relevant to all transactions, the following summarizes most of the key business terms that arise when negotiating with lenders.

Loan Maturity Date—Real estate investors need to ensure that their loans are long enough to provide sufficient time to complete their investment objectives. A five-year loan with a 30-year amortization schedule is still a five-year loan and will need to be repaid in full in five years.

I have seen numerous real estate investors borrow money for a specific period of time based upon their estimated project timelines. Then market conditions changed or the project got delayed for one or more reasons. When the borrowers tried to refinance their projects, they could no longer find willing lenders and were forced to default on their loans. Always add some conservatism when assessing your needed financing time frames.

Amortization Schedule—The amount of any scheduled principal amortization will affect the amount of your periodic payments. A shorter amortization period results in larger payments but also reduces the amount of your loan balance more quickly. A longer amortization schedule reduces your payments but results in a higher loan balance over time.

Traditional residential housing loans have the most simplistic amortization schedules. A 15-year fixed rate loan has a 15-year amortization schedule. A 30-year loan has a 30-year amortization schedule. If a borrower makes his monthly payments for 15 or 30 years, on the last payment date, his loan will have a balance of zero and be completely repaid.

Other more complex loan products will allow longer amortization schedules with shorter term loans. For example, a seven-year loan might have an amortization schedule of 20 years. At the end of seven years, the outstanding principal balance of the loan is due in full. This results in what is referred to as a "balloon" payment, which is essentially the unamortized portion of your loan balance that is due to your lender on the loan's maturity date.

Some loans have no scheduled amortization and only require a borrower to make interest payments until the end of the loan when the entire principal balance is due. Many land acquisition loans are structured this way. Other loans may allow some or all of the periodic interest due on the loan to accrue and be payable at the end of the loan. For example, I recently reviewed a loan with a 12.5% annual interest rate that allowed the borrower to pay 8% interest per year in cash and pay the remaining 4.5% of accrued interest in two years when the loan matured.

As indicated in Chapter 4, "The Benefits and Risks of Leverage," borrowing money from other people can substantially increase the profitability of an investment. This is why I normally try to negotiate the longest amortization schedule possible (if any at all). I want my monthly payments to be low and I want to maximize my leverage so why would I want to repay my loans early?

But sometimes I can negotiate a significantly lower interest rate when I agree to a shorter amortization schedule. In such cases, I use a financial model to tell me which financing option will produce the most projected profit.

Interest Rate—The lower your interest rate, the greater the profitability of your investment. In order to get the lowest interest rate, you usually have to request financing from more than one lender. Also, do not be shy toward letting potential lenders know that they are competing against at least one of their peers. I try not to give the impression that a lender is one of many so that each lender believes that he has a strong chance of winning the lending opportunity. But I do want them to put their best foot forward and knowing that there is competition usually helps.

If given a choice between a fixed rate of interest and an adjustable or "floating" rate of interest, consider your investment timeline and make sure that you have ample cash flow to make the required payments. Usually, adjustable rate loans have lower initial interest rates when compared to fixed rate loans. However, with adjustable rate loans, you run the risk that future interest rates will rise significantly and that over time your adjustable rate of interest will become higher than what you would have been paying with a fixed interest rate loan.

Many borrowers have lost property to lenders, have been forced into bankruptcy, and have experienced other financial difficulties due to rising loan payments caused by adjustable rates of interest. These rate increases result when interest rates reset on certain dates. For example, an adjustable rate loan may require the borrower to pay a fixed rate of 5% for the first five years, then reset at the start of the sixth year to a rate equal to 2.5% plus the current interest rate on a two-year government note. The borrower does not know what the interest rate on the two-year government note will be in five years. If it ends up being 6%, the interest rate on the borrower's loan will change from 5% to 8.5%. Such a dramatic move can place financial distress on an investment and cause a borrower to default on his loan.

The rise and fall of the residential housing market that has recently taken place can be substantially blamed on the aggressive lending policies employed by lenders and the ignorance or denial of many borrowers. Creating loans that borrowers could only afford with very low initial interest rates knowing that these rates would rise dramatically in the near future was imprudent. Lenders and borrowers should have ensured that higher payments, that in many cases were certain to occur, could be afforded.

Loan Origination Fees or "Points"—Lenders will often charge an up-front origination fee on real estate loans. Origination fees are quoted as a percentage of the principal balance of the loan. For example, a loan origination fee of 1% (which equals "one point") on a $200,000 loan would equate to an up-front fee of $2,000. Every point equals 1% of the loan principal balance.

These fees vary based upon the type of property you are trying to finance, the current lending environment, and the specific type of lender. I have seen origination fees range from 0% to 5%. Borrowers may avoid any origination fees on loans secured by residential properties. This is more likely in competitive lending markets in which banks are aggressively trying to lend money. In more conservative lending environments, lenders have more negotiating power and are able to charge higher financing costs.

You might expect to pay 0.5% to 1% on commercial property loans. The stronger the collateral, the more negotiating room you should have. For example, a commercial property having a long-term lease to a credit-worthy tenant provides greater comfort to a lender than a property that is only partially completed and that generates no income.

When borrowing money against riskier properties such as raw land, borrowers can often expect to pay several points. Sometimes these fees are allocated between different parties involved in arranging the financing. For example, if a broker is used, the broker may earn one point and the lender providing the actual money might earn two points.

Borrowers are sometimes presented with multiple financing options for a particular piece of property. Such choices can come from the same lender or from multiple lenders. In return for higher up-front origination fees, lenders are often willing to accept lower interest rates on a loan.

Table 9.1 shows a simplistic example of what a lender might offer to a potential borrower. As you can see, for a $500,000 loan the lender is willing to lower the interest rate in return for higher origination fees. One of the reasons for this compromise is that many loans are prepaid before their maturity dates. As you can see, Option 3 results in the lowest financing cost when the loan remains

Table 9.1
Lender Financing Scenarios

Term	Option 1	Option 2	Option 3
Loan amount	$ 500,000	$ 500,000	$ 500,000
Points	0.00%	1.00%	2.50%
Interest rate	7.00%	6.50%	6.00%
Loan maturity date	5 years	5 years	5 years
Financing costs—5 years			
Points	$ –	$ 5,000	$ 12,500
Interest for 5 years	175,000	162,500	150,000
Total financing costs	$ 175,000	$ 167,500	$ 162,500
Financing costs—3 years			
Points	$ –	$ 5,000	$ 12,500
Interest for 5 years	105,000	97,500	90,000
Total financing costs	$ 105,000	$ 102,500	$ 102,500
Financing costs—1 year			
Points	$ –	$ 5,000	$ 12,500
Interest for 5 years	35,000	32,500	30,000
Total financing costs	$ 35,000	$ 37,500	$ 42,500

outstanding for its full five-year term. However, Option 3 also has the highest financing cost if the loan is repaid after one year.

Borrowers need to consider their financing needs when determining whether to pay higher loan origination fees, which is often referred to as "buying down the interest rate" because paying a higher up-front origination fee effectively buys a lower interest rate on the loan. Borrowers should also consider the "time value of money" when reviewing differing loan terms. Remember that dollars paid today are worth more to the recipient than dollars received later.

Borrowers should ask for multiple financing options and the more options the better. So be sure to ask your lenders to provide as many choices as possible. Look for options regarding terms such as loan maturity date, the amortization schedule, and ranging interest rates and origination fees and choose the best financing structure for your particular needs.

Loan-to-Value—Lenders limit the amount of money that they will lend based upon a loan-to-value or "LTV" ratio. When determining how much to lend, lenders start by assessing the value of the property that you own or are preparing to purchase by ordering an appraisal. If a single-family house is appraised at $200,000 and a lender is willing to lend using an 80% LTV ratio, then you can borrow $160,000 against this property. You will need to cover the other $40,000 plus any closing costs.

In aggressive lending markets, some lenders may be willing to lend closer to 100% against the appraised value of a property. In tighter and more conservative lending environments, such as the one now underway due to the residential housing market turmoil, it becomes much more difficult to obtain financing and LTV ratios tend to be substantially more conservative (i.e., 80% or less).

Assuming your investment is earning more over time than the cost of the money that you have borrowed, the higher the LTV ratio, the greater the profitability of the investment. Of course, this assumes that you can make any required periodic payments on the debt. Many people have lost great investments because they borrowed too much money and could not keep their payments current.

When an investment is earning less than the cost of your borrowings, using other people's money to finance your investment will lower investment profitability and often result in losses. Investments that lose money will lose even more money when borrowed funds are employed.

Personal Guarantees—Sometimes lenders are unwilling to lend solely against the value of a property and want further assurances that they will be repaid. In such cases, a lender may require you to sign a personal guarantee. Under a personal guarantee, if you default on a loan obligation and a lender is forced to take your property as collateral, you agree to cover any shortfall through other means. For example, if you borrowed $100 against a property and are unable to make the monthly payments, your lender will initiate foreclosure proceedings and take ownership and possession of the property. If the property is only worth $80, the lender is going to require you to pay the remaining $20. You may have to sell other assets or establish some form of payment plan in order to satisfy this obligation.

Most residential housing loans require personal guarantees whether or not the property is serving as an owner's residence or as an investment. Sometimes residential housing investors are able to accumulate enough properties and build up enough financial strength within a borrowing entity so that personal guarantees can be avoided. This may be the case when many investors pool their capital by investing in a company that owns real estate. However, many lenders may still require personal guarantees from one or more of the investors.

Avoiding personal guarantees when borrowing against commercial property is more common, but many lenders still require such assurances. I often see lenders that are originating commercial loans for securitization rely solely on the value of the collateral and not require personal guarantees. Sometimes local lenders will be so comfortable with one or more properties that they will not require a guarantee as well. Such determinations vary by lender and by the overall lending market. When lenders are competing against one another and eager to lend money, borrower terms become more flexible.

My advice is to try to avoid giving personal guarantees whenever possible. This can be a negotiation topic when speaking to and comparing multiple lenders. When you do give a personal guarantee, be certain that your investment will retain enough of its value under severe circumstances to cover your loan balance.

Make sure you can make your payments under differing real estate cycles, interest rate environments, etc. This might mean borrowing less and giving up a portion of the potential profitability of an investment due to lesser leverage, but such risk aversion may be a smarter decision.

Financial Covenants—Often times lenders will require borrowers to maintain minimum levels of financial strength to ensure that they have the ability to continue making payments and ultimately repay their loans. To monitor a borrower's financial condition and to protect the lender's position, borrowers are sometimes required to meet or exceed certain financial covenants.

The exact terms and calculations of financial covenants are highly negotiable and can vary dramatically by borrower and lender. Sometimes the borrower is required to compute these calculations and other times the lender will do so internally and a borrower may never see the results (unless the borrower defaults on one or more covenants). In order to compute financial covenants, borrowers must prepare financial statements. At the very least, this usually requires a balance sheet and an income statement for the borrower and potentially any additional loan guarantors.

A local accountant or accounting firm can prepare financial statements for borrowers. This is usually done on a quarterly or annual basis. Sometimes lenders will require a third-party accountant to provide a formal written opinion that your financial statements are in compliance with Generally Accepted Accounting Principles (GAAP) to ensure that there are no material errors in the numbers. These would be considered "audited" financial statements, which usually involve more work by the accountant and result in higher costs. In some cases, lenders will allow "unaudited" financial statements prepared by the borrower. This decision is usually based upon your relationship with the lender, the lender's confidence in your ability to prepare accurate financial statements and the specific type of property and overall perceived risk of the loan.

Typical financial covenants might include Maximum Leverage (to ensure a borrower does not assume too much debt), Minimum Tangible Net Worth (to make sure that a borrower's net worth does not drop below a certain level), and a Debt Service Coverage Ratio (to monitor a borrower or investment's ability to generate enough cash to cover its expenses and debt payments). There are many other types of financial covenants that can be tailored to a specific type of borrower, property, or industry. I will not try to explain the specific calculations. As mentioned, the formulas for such covenants can vary significantly and are highly negotiable.

As with personal guarantees, financial covenants place more risk on a borrower and should be avoided whenever possible. When financial covenants are being considered and negotiated, borrowers should make sure that they understand how to perform the calculations and how movements in certain variables and in the performance of one or more investments will ultimately affect the covenant results. You should strive to make sure that you can remain compliant with your financial covenants under multiple adverse scenarios.

In the unfortunate circumstance in which you violate one or more financial covenants, do not immediately give up on your investment and expect to lose your property. Banks and other lenders would much rather receive their money back than be forced to take ownership of a property under a defaulted loan.

Sometimes lenders are willing to renegotiate financial covenants when needed. The more proactive you can be and the more notice you can provide to a lender the better. If you feel confident that you are going to violate a financial covenant, meet with your lender quickly and candidly discuss your situation and express your openness to alternative solutions.

Events of Default—In order to protect a lender's investment, almost all loan documents will include a listing of possible "Events of Default." Triggering one of these items usually allows the lender to require all interest and principal owed on a loan to become due and payable immediately. Obviously, this is an unfavorable occurrence that can ruin the profitability of an investment and have adverse repercussions for a borrower. Such outcomes can include loss of properties and any additional pledged collateral to lenders, the requirement to pay additional proceeds under personal guarantees, and poor credit and the inability to borrow in the future.

The most common and certain Event of Default is lack of timely payment. If you are obligated to make a payment to a bank each month and you stop doing so, this would clearly result in an Event of Default and allow the lender to require full repayment of the entire loan immediately. Other Events of Default might include violation of financial covenants, bankruptcy, the death or mental incompetence of a borrower or guarantor, and failure to provide required reports on time (e.g., quarterly or annual financial statements or tax returns). In addition, if a lender determines that something you previously stated is untrue (e.g., materially overstated financial statements), you may also be in default.

Some of the less severe Events of Default often provide cure periods. For example, while missing a loan payment is a serious act and can result in immediate default, missing a reporting deadline is not as meaningful. In such cases, borrowers often have a certain number of days (i.e., 30 calendar days) to fix the problem and remain in compliance. These are negotiation points when documenting a loan that attorneys can be helpful with.

As with financial covenants, you want to ensure that you have ample room within the parameters of your loan documents to operate without coming close to triggering any Events of Default. Stress your investment and financial condition assuming adverse circumstances and be confident that any lender requirements are not too stringent. If you do trigger an Event of Default or know that you will ultimately do so, contact your lender, be proactive, and try to find a win-win solution while there may still be available alternatives.

Prepayment Penalties—Lenders like when borrowers borrow money. The more good loans that a lender makes, the more money the lender earns. When borrowers repay their loans, lenders need to relend the money to someone else.

Obtaining approval for a loan and completing the documentation and other administrative functions consume lender resources. A lender does not want you to take a five-year loan and then repay it after only a few months. Unless the lender is charging a substantial up-front origination fee, providing such short-term loans does not make sense. Some lenders charge (or attempt to charge) prepayment penalties on certain loans to protect themselves from such early repayments.

Under other circumstances, prepayment penalties are charged to compensate a lender for lower general market interest rates at the time a loan is prepaid versus when the loan was originally made. For example, assume that you get a five-year loan with a fixed interest rate of 8% and that you prepay the loan after two years. Also assume that two years later, when you prepay your loan, the bank can only make a similar loan at 6% due to lower market interest rates. Now the bank will earn less money on its new loan. To compensate the bank for this risk, the bank may require a prepayment penalty.

Generic loans on residential properties usually do not have prepayment penalties, but I have seen some customized residential loans contain such provisions. An example of such a circumstance might be for a loan to someone that is self-employed with a volatile source of income and weak credit strength. A local bank might agree to provide this type of borrower a loan, but at a higher interest rate and with more customized terms.

A simplistic prepayment penalty might be a fee of 1% times the outstanding principal balance of the loan at the time of prepayment. For example, if you owed $100,000 and prepaid the loan, you would be forced to pay a prepayment penalty of $1,000. Other prepayment penalty calculations can be much more complicated and be based on variables such as the interest rate on a specific government bond at the time of prepayment. In such cases, the penalty amount can vary each day. During very-low-interest-rate environments, I have seen some prepayment penalties equal 40% or more of the outstanding loan amount.

Normally prepayment penalties only cover a certain period of time and become less stringent over the term of the loan. For example, there may be a 1% prepayment penalty on a 10-year loan during the first three years. After such time the borrower can prepay without any additional costs. Another type of prepayment penalty might require a 5% penalty in the first year of the loan, a 4% penalty for the second year, a 3% penalty for the third year, and so on.

Floating rate loans usually do not have prepayment penalties, while many commercial fixed rate loan documents contain such provisions. Commercial fixed rate loans that are intended for securitization usually have the most stringent prepayment provisions in order to compensate the underlying bondholders for early repayment and to make the bonds more marketable to investors. Loans from local banks usually have the most attractive prepayment penalties (if any).

As with most loan terms, prepayment penalties are often negotiable. As a real estate investor, you want to maintain as much flexibility as possible. Having the right to prepay a loan at anytime is helpful when choosing to sell or refinance a property. Try your best to avoid such provisions whenever possible. If you do agree to a prepayment penalty, make sure that you are getting something favorable in return, such as a substantially lower interest rate. In addition, consider your investment horizon. If you plan to buy and sell a property within the next two years, you do not want a prepayment penalty on your loan for the next five years.

SUMMARY

Depending upon a particular lending environment, obtaining financing for a specific property acquisition or refinancing can be more or less difficult. When banks take significant losses on real estate loans, they tend to overreact and become ultraconservative or even stop such lending completely. Other times in strong markets when lenders are eager to lend money, heavy competition results and borrowers can negotiate extremely favorable terms.

But when real estate financing is scarce and lenders are being overly conservative, the prices of real estate tend to fall dramatically. With fewer buyers in the market able to obtain financing, the supply tends to outweigh the demand for properties. Such circumstances present great buying opportunities for real estate investors.

Impress your lenders by being well prepared and by acting professionally. Continue to build a strong and credible network of capital providers. Be prepared to invest more equity and receive less debt financing in down markets. A prudent real estate investor is one that can adapt to current market conditions and gather the appropriate resources needed to invest within all market cycles.

Chapter 10

WORKING WITH THIRD PARTIES

I do not claim to be an expert on any subject. I try to maintain enough knowledge regarding the various investments that I own to make prudent decisions. If I do not feel confident in my level of experience in a specific area, I either choose not to invest or trust the expertise of a specialist.

RECOGNIZE YOUR LIMITATIONS

After making mistakes and misunderstanding topics for which I was ill-trained fairly earlier in my career, I learned the importance of having a team of advisors. These are the people that spend their entire careers focused upon narrow fields that require ongoing knowledge of markets and many detailed rules and laws. These are the people that stay up-to-date on the ongoing changes within their industries and how these changes affect the businesses of their clients. Examples of such professionals include Realtors, mortgage brokers and lenders, property managers, tax advisors and attorneys, inspection companies, and other industry professionals.

By maintaining relationships with industry experts, you have a better chance of being proactive rather than reactive when it comes to key business decisions. Knowledge is truly an asset that differentiates the novice from the expert. Do not be afraid to ask for help and do not let your ego dominate your decisions. I am quick to admit when my limitations have been reached and when guidance from an industry specialist is needed.

Some service providers are clearly better than others and often times it takes awhile to find the best people. When working for a real estate management company, I remember firing two accounting firms over a three-year period until I found a third that provided an acceptable level of service. I also fired a tax advisor and an attorney during the same period. The better your service providers, the better you can expect your business ventures to perform.

While cost savings are always important, sometimes you get what you pay for. Make sure that you are receiving excellent expertise even if you are paying a higher price for such services. For example, having your tax return prepared annually by a franchised accounting firm that assigns a different person to your account each year is not a wise decision. Having a relationship with a personal tax advisor for many years that understands your specific investments and objectives will provide much greater benefits.

Before continuing, let me say that I recognize that the fees of professional service providers can be excessive. I often get frustrated when I see a legal bill detailing conversations between my attorney and I that lasted only five minutes, especially when I consider all the work that I provide and refer to him. Some service professionals will bill by the hour, while others will bill by the project or task at hand. I usually prefer the latter.

As a small real estate investor just getting started or one with only a small property or two, I am not suggesting that you go out and hire a large staff of people or place numerous professional firms on retainer. Rather, be aware of the benefits that such individuals can provide and use them selectively when needed. Over time, the better service providers will become apparent.

THE VALUE OF A NETWORK

Having industry professionals know and like you can be a very powerful resource. For example, Realtors are always seeking property buyers and sellers. If you have relationships with Realtors that know your targeted regions and property types and believe that you have reliable financing available, be assured that they will be bringing deals to your attention. If they know of a property owner that wants to sell quickly and is willing to take a price concession to do so, you may be presented with a winning property acquisition. Think of all the time and effort this can save you. Looking at properties can be very time consuming and frustrating, particularly in up markets when high prices often do not make sense.

Providing industry professionals with your business is clearly a way to get their attention. But not only can you build solid relationships with such people by paying them fees for the services they provide, you can also win their loyalty and appreciation by referring other clients to them. When I trust and respect an industry professional, I will recommend his services at every opportunity. I do this as a favor to the people seeking such services, but also as a means to strengthen my network. I am sure to tell people when contacting one of my relationships to mention that I referred their services.

Networking is a significant part of business and investing. I see this time and time again. People tend to favor clients that provide them direct and indirect business opportunities. When short on time, I can usually get my lawyer or tax advisor to immediately focus on my requests regardless of how busy they are. By being trustworthy, respectful, and fair, and most importantly, a great reference and a source of income for my network members, the quality of the service I receive is increased. In addition, I sometimes receive discounts and I am often referred business and investing opportunities.

Building and maintaining relationships with a collection of industry professionals can be inexpensive and very rewarding. Consider this to be a side job affiliated with your real estate investing. Refer good people to others and such favors will be reciprocated. Refer people that you like, trust, and admire and focus on these character traits within your own business activities. Maintain proper ethics and business principles throughout all aspects of your life. Be honest, keep people informed so that they are not caught off guard, pay your bills on time, and do not mislead anyone. Doing the right thing, considering other people's feelings and perspectives, and paying attention to your actions can payoff by manyfold.

Now let us discuss some of the most relevant professions within the real estate industry. While this list is not all-inclusive, it should reference most of the key players that you should strive to include within your network.

REALTORS

I shared some of my views on Realtors in a prior chapter. Particularly within the residential real estate markets, the range between good and bad Realtors is enormous. I watched countless people switch careers and become Realtors during the most recent housing market madness. Anyone that could read and take a simple test seemed to be obtaining a license. But the quality of commercial Realtors can widely vary as well. As with any profession, some individuals and firms are far better than others.

In the late 1990s and early 2000s, my wife was managing a collection of rental properties for our own portfolio. I sometimes became involved with the negotiations when she was buying and selling properties. I was stunned by the lack of service and limited expertise that Realtors were exhibiting when working for their clients. My two primary disappointments related to a general level of incompetence and a lack of motivation.

There are many Realtors that have been in the industry for many years and even decades and have amassed a significant amount of experience. These people understand the various selling techniques that become more or less relevant within a given market cycle. They know the meaning and importance or unimportance of specific contract terms. They have seen and used the better negotiation tactics. These are competent Realtors.

But competence can sometimes be limiting. Just because a Realtor has the proper skill set and knows what should be done for the betterment of his client does not mean he will always do so. Not only do you want an overly competent Realtor, you also want one that is hungry for business and motivated to serve clients and enhance his reputation.

Remember that Realtors are paid by commission and commission-based pay can often result in conflicts of interest. If a Realtor is earning a 3% commission to sell a property, it is often easier to passively handle an offer rather than fight for a higher selling price and risk losing or delaying a sale.

Sometimes people age and slow down, particularly when retirement is approaching. Other times they have too many preoccupations. For example, being a Realtor and raising a family is challenging. Maybe a Realtor has too many other property listings and clients and cannot devote enough time to each one. Maybe there is more focus on higher priced properties that generate greater commissions. It is important to find Realtors that are motivated and that will be properly focused on your specific property.

Realtor commissions are normally paid by the seller of a property. There is a listing agent, which is the Realtor responsible for marketing and ensuring that other Realtors and potential buyers are aware of the property and its attractiveness. Then there is often a buyer's agent, which is the Realtor representing a buyer of a property. These two roles are sometimes performed by the same Realtor. For example, a Realtor may be engaged by a seller to list a property and then ultimately be the one that finds a buyer as well. Such duel roles can present further conflicts of interest as one Realtor is representing two opposing parties.

Realtor commissions are negotiated between the Realtor representing the seller and the seller. Commissions can vary depending on property type and market conditions. In a slow residential housing market, you might see commissions of 5–7%. Of this amount, the seller's agent and the buyer's agent may share these fees equally (i.e., 2.5–3.5% each). In a more attractive housing market, you might be able to negotiate total commissions between 4% and 5%.

In commercial markets, commissions can vary based upon a property's value, the state of the market, its location, and the size of the property. Typical commissions for small multifamily and commercial properties are often in the 3–5% range. Larger commercial properties may have commissions ranging from 1% to 3%. Larger properties can result in lower commission percentages since the total commission can be so significant. As with residential properties, the better the market, the lower commissions that can be negotiated. In more challenging markets with fewer buyers and more properties for sale, higher commissions usually result.

When selling properties and negotiating commissions, you clearly want to save money by receiving a fair commission agreement, but also remember that you want to motivate the buy side and sell side Realtors (more importantly, the buyer's Realtor). Sales-based commissions can affect the marketability of a property. For example, if a Realtor is helping a buyer to find a property, he might consciously or subconsciously avoid or deter the buyer from buying a property that pays a 2% commission versus another property that pays 3%.

Because commissions are often shared between a Realtor and his employer, I sometimes offer special bonuses to a buyer's Realtor (e.g., $5,000) when selling a property because such a bonus is often not shared between the Realtor and his employer. Such bonuses are more common in down markets. When selling a property, talk to your listing agent about structuring an appropriate buy-side commission. For example, it is not unusual to see a selling Realtor receive a 2% commission while the buyer's Realtor receives a 3% commission on the same property. In addition, if the seller's Realtor lists the property for sale, but also finds a buyer, a lower total commission could be agreed upon, such as 4%.

When choosing a Realtor to sell your property, be sure to interview different people, ask others for referrals, and focus on experience and motivation. Such experience should pertain to the type of property you are selling (i.e., residential or commercial, high or low price range, etc.), its location, and the state of the current real estate market. Motivation is a unique quality that is more subjectively defined. Look for high-energy people that have many ideas about how to sell your property.

Once you find one or more good Realtors that have proven their abilities, build long-term relationships and use them as often as possible (assuming appropriate for your objectives) and remember to refer other potential clients to them. As mentioned, Realtors can be a great resource. Let them know when you are seeking to acquire properties. Also, when they know which properties you own, they may bring you potential buyers. You may not be thinking about selling, but at the right price you may change your mind.

Some real estate investors earn their real estate licenses so that they can pay lower purchase prices by earning commissions when buying a property and avoiding a portion of commissions when selling properties. However, Realtors must be employed by a real estate broker in order for their licenses to be active. Such employers will usually want a portion of any commission earned in return. Depending upon the level of your real estate investing, you may want to pursue a broker's license, although doing so will result in additional expenses such as insurance and other costs.

MORTGAGE BROKERS AND LENDERS

We have discussed some of the benefits of having well-established relationships with mortgage brokers and lenders. To justify such relationships, they need to know that you are a serious investor and that you are honest and reliable. If you continue to bring them deals that never manifest or if you renege on promises, then you will never establish trust and credibility.

Regarding lenders, you need to know that your loan requests will be handled promptly and given a high probability of acceptance. You also need to feel comfortable that you are being provided with fair and reasonable terms. You do not want a loan broker that is going to try to charge you an excessive interest rate that has to be materially negotiated downward every time you apply for a loan.

As mentioned, having the ability to obtain interest rate quotes quickly helps to assess a property's profitability when considering a bid. Having preapproved financing can strengthen your negotiating position and sometimes convince sellers to lower their prices in return for a rapid and reliable closing. Obtaining preapproval for financing is a more reasonable expectation when purchasing residential homes, since these types of properties are more generic than most commercial properties. However, based upon your lender relationships and assuming you are not significantly overpaying or buying properties that you cannot afford, you should have a good idea about whether you qualify to buy a certain commercial property.

Mortgage brokers and lenders can also be a great resource. By being such active industry participants, these professionals come across numerous opportunities such as willing buyers and distressed property owners that need to sell fast. In addition, they are a great source of industry information since they frequently see so many transactions.

PROPERTY MANAGERS

Depending upon how involved you intend to be with the properties you own, you may or may not want to employ the services of a property manager. A property manager is responsible for finding tenants, collecting rent, overseeing needed repairs and maintenance, and general accounting. Using such a service can reduce the number of headaches that you might experience, but having such a luxury comes at a cost.

Often it is difficult for property owners to manage their properties in an unbiased and professional manner. This is understandable considering that you own the property and that you are directly paying for most of the associated costs. If you choose to take on this role, try to maintain a "business is business" attitude and make prudent decisions that are best for your investment.

Property managers need to have good interpersonal skills and maintain professionalism. Not only do property managers have to deal with current tenants, they also have to meet and interact with prospective tenants. This is often done on weekends for residential properties.

If you are willing to show properties to prospective tenants, collect rents, and call repair people when needed, you may choose not to pay the expense associated with a property management firm. If you are willing and able to perform the repairs yourself, you can save even more money. It all depends on your level of comfort and how involved you want to be.

Paying a property manager for at least the first year is not such a bad idea. Such firms can be a significant resource by creating your first lease, giving you market feedback before purchase, handling repairs and evictions, etc. If you do choose to manage property yourself, I recommend that you consult an experienced real estate attorney if you are ever forced to evict a tenant or if you encounter any other problems that could have legal implications.

Serving as your own property manager for residential and small commercial properties is feasible and a matter of personal choice. If your properties become larger and more complex, the use of a property manager becomes almost mandatory. Commercial property leases can get very complicated and include such items as tenant improvement allowances, scheduled rental increases, and cost responsibility and sharing arrangements. In addition, the maintenance and repair aspects warrant someone experienced in such matters.

The typical fees for property management depend primarily on property type and size. Most fees are based upon a percentage of the income generated by a property, while other firms will perform this service for a flat monthly fee. Paying a percentage of income motivates a property manager to keep rents at market rates. Generally, lower management fee percentages will be charged on larger properties. A fee of 8–10% of gross rents is normal on residential properties. Such fees might range from 3% to 8% for commercial properties depending upon their size and complexity.

Additional fees may be required for leasing vacant space due to the additional work involved when preparing a rental property for use and for marketing the property and finding the tenants. For residential properties, this may be a flat fee or a percentage, such as 50% of the first month's rent. For commercial properties, such fees are usually a percentage of the ongoing rent with such fees declining over time.

Property managers can be a great addition to your team. They can free up a substantial amount of your time and allow you to pursue other activities. Your decision to use a property management firm should be based upon your desired amount of involvement, your personality and appropriate skill levels, and the number, type, and complexity of your properties.

Just like when choosing a Realtor or other team member, the property management selection process should include researching and interviewing several service providers. Seek referrals and consider the type of expertise of each firm. Do not use a property management firm that specializes in commercial property for your residential properties and vice versa. Obtain a listing of fees for each service provided (i.e., leasing vacant units, ongoing property management, etc.) and do not hesitate to ask for pricing discounts in advance particularly as your portfolio of properties grows.

THE TAX ADVISOR

Tax is a complicated field that requires specialists that focus solely on tax matters and nothing else. I meet with my tax advisor frequently for a number of purposes. Rather than looking for qualifying deductions for my tax return after the tax year is over like many taxpayers, I meet with my advisor and determine which deductions I should be aware of and targeting before the tax year even begins. In addition, before buying or selling a real estate investment, I make sure that I know the resulting tax consequences or I consult with my tax advisor before doing so. To act first and hope for the best later is counterproductive. There is little a tax advisor can do for you once you have closed a transaction.

When I use the term "tax advisor," I am not referring to a franchised CPA firm that spits out thousands of tax returns in the first few months of the year. In many cases, these people are serving more of a robotic role of entering numbers and printing your tax return after the tax year has ended. You want someone that you can build a relationship with and that understands your investment holdings and your overall objectives.

A tax advisor can let you know if your real estate activities will qualify under active participation rules which will determine whether or not you can receive certain tax benefits. In addition, he can let you know the type of tax treatment that a certain investment will receive. For example, projects entailing construction and development activities usually require an investor to pay income taxes on any profits at ordinary tax rates, while more passive investments can allow income to be taxed at a lower capital gains tax rate.

Tax advisors can also aid you in structuring "like-kind exchanges." Internal Revenue Code Section 1031 allows qualifying investors to sell an investment property and defer the payment of income taxes if they purchase another investment property within a predefined period of time. For example, if you sell a property for which you paid $100,000 three years ago for $150,000, normally you would be forced to pay income taxes on the $50,000 gain. However, under

Section 1031, if you reinvest the sales proceeds into a new real estate investment, you can avoid this tax payment until you sell the second property (or you can keep reinvesting in additional like-kind exchanges and continue to defer tax payments). Additional tax benefits can be received by investors that can qualify as real estate professionals.

There is a cost for a tax advisor's time, but I am confident that the advice provided will be well worth an hour or two of consultation fees. As with all service providers, some tax advisors are much better than others, so be selective and focus on building a relationship with a tax advisor that spends a lot of his time working with real estate.

REAL ESTATE ATTORNEYS

As your properties grow in complexity and number, your need to have a real estate attorney within your network becomes more likely. When purchasing generic residential properties, the documentation and closing process is fairly simplistic. An experienced Realtor can be a great advisor for such transactions. In addition, a reputable property management firm can aid you in structuring leases that adhere to specific state rules and that provide market terms and landlord protections.

In some states, a real estate attorney is used to serve as the closing agent for a transaction. This role is to coordinate the signing of all the documents, obtain title insurance on the property, ensure the payment of all relevant state taxes, properly oversee the division of costs, and facilitate the movement of funds between buyer, seller, and their lenders. In other states, it is more common to use a title company to perform these services.

When dealing with larger residential and commercial properties, particularly having multiple tenants and varying lease structures, I strongly recommend the use of a qualified real estate attorney. Your attorney should review purchase- and sales-related documents, as well as any financing documents. Your financing may rely on existing or future leases as collateral, you may be assuming debt with the purchase of the property, and the terms of more complex loans can require substantial negotiation. In addition, you need to be sure that all existing and future leases associated with a property are properly written.

Similar to when using the services of a tax advisor, be sure to consult with your attorney before finalizing a transaction. The majority of the value that a real estate attorney provides is before the final documents are signed. Look for one or more attorneys that specialize in real estate and leasing transactions.

PROPERTY INSPECTION FIRMS

You will need to engage consultants regardless of the scope or complexity of your real estate activities. The primary purpose of using consultants is to assess any problems associated with a property. Buying a property without knowing any major hidden defects is similar to buying a used car without having a mechanic review its current condition. But as you might expect, the costs associated with a defective piece of real estate can dwarf those of a defective automobile.

One of the most important consultants that you will use each time you purchase a property is a structural inspection firm. My advice is to always order an inspection before buying a property even if the property is brand new. Do not settle for a home inspection ordered by a seller.

When purchasing residential properties, do not agree to a home warranty in replace of your own inspection. Home warranties have countless provisions that allow the insurer to avoid covering many repairs. In addition, there are significant deductibles that often apply.

Commercial properties often have deferred maintenance, meaning that the seller has chosen not to make one or more material repair or maintenance expenditures. Such items might include resealing parking facilities, new roofing, pool and deck resurfacing, painting, and new carpeting. These are all expenses that you will be forced to endure as the property's new owner. An inspection can be invaluable in identifying such items and serve to strengthen your negotiating position.

The cost of an inspection usually pays for itself many times over. The report you receive should identify any problems associated with the property. Some of these items may be material such as the need for a new roof or heating and air conditioning system. Others will be less material, but these are all items that should be addressed by the seller either through price concessions or by making the actual repairs. When a substantial amount of repairs are being made by the seller, pay the inspection firm to revisit the property and review the outcome to ensure compliance.

Sometimes the results of an inspection will be a deal breaker. The seller either refuses to admit that such problems exist or is unwilling to undertake the additional costs or lower his sales price. In such cases, it is sometimes best to walk away and move on to the next potential property. In other cases, you may be getting such a great deal that you are willing to compromise. All contracts should be contingent upon the receipt of having an inspection performed on the property. If the potential sale is terminated due to the inspection results, any buyer deposits should be fully refundable.

Another type of inspection is often needed to assess any property damage caused by pests and organisms that destroy wood and other building materials. Examples include damage caused by termites, carpenter ants, and other wood-destroying insects. Often indications of such damage can be seen visually and may be picked up by your structural inspection. However, unless you are looking at a wood-sided property, most of the wood is within the walls and other crevices. I normally consult my structural inspector to determine the need for any pest inspection. Also, the specific property and its location play a key role. If I am looking at a wood-framed house in Florida where insects are prevalent, I will order a pest inspection. If I am buying a block-framed property in a dryer climate, I might not.

A mold inspection may be needed for properties that have experienced some form of water intrusion. Usually if events such as plumbing leaks and flooding are cleaned up and treated quickly, such problems can be avoided. The existence of mold can cause respiratory problems for occupants and lead to a slew of unwanted headaches and expenses. A decision to order a mold inspection report will be driven by the specific property type, its location and history.

OTHER INDUSTRY PROFESSIONALS

If your investing activities expand, you may be required to use the services of other consultants. For example, when purchasing commercial properties, most lenders will require you to order a Phase I environmental report. If the Phase I reports shows any potential problems, a Phase II environmental report is required to determine whether there is any contamination. You will also want this information for your own peace of mind. Be cognizant of specific types of tenants such as gas stations, dry cleaners, and other operators using hazardous materials. These occupants may have resided on your targeted property or on nearby properties.

You will want to develop a relationship with one or more insurance agents. The better insurance agents will have extensive experience dealing with residential and commercial policies. Even if you only own residential properties, you may be able to wrap all of your properties into one commercial policy that will provide significant cost savings. I have found the better insurance agents to be less driven by commissions and more focused on finding the best products for their clients (such people are not easy to find!). Your lender will usually research whether or not the property you are buying is in a flood zone. If so, you will most likely be required to purchase flood insurance, which should be another consideration when forecasting a property's profitability.

Appraisals usually need to be ordered directly by your lender. However, often times you may choose a specific appraiser on a lender's approved list of service providers. An appraiser can provide a wealth of information about a specific property and market. Whether you have a relationship with a specific appraiser or not, I encourage you to speak to such professionals whenever the opportunity arises. For example, when a bank orders an appraisal on your property, ask if you can speak to the appraiser to gain a better understanding of the process. Ask him what he thinks about the property and the surrounding areas, its future prospects, and ways to increase its value.

There are many other types of consultants that can be very useful depending upon your particular investment objectives and targeted properties. If considering a purchase or the start of new construction, you may want a demographic study performed to assess the attractiveness of a retail site. You might want to know historic traffic patterns, the types and incomes of the residents in the area, and any competition recently completed or approved for development.

At other times, you may want to pay a consultant to research and help you to obtain specific tax credits or find you the right financing for a complicated project. Maybe you want to understand the benefits and necessary hurdles in developing energy-efficient property. The list of possibilities is quite extensive. Just know that when you have a particular need, there is most likely an industry specialist somewhere that can help you.

SUMMARY

You might be surprised by how much business is generated through referrals and how small a local community can seem when everyone knows everyone in a specific market. Getting to know such industry professionals can help you to find the best service providers and obtain inside knowledge about specific properties and markets. The best way to truly learn about the value drivers within a local area is to talk to the people that have and continue to work within these real estate markets every day.

Your network can also generate opportunities, including identifying properties for sale and potential property buyers. Many property purchases and sales take place without the general public's knowledge. Sometimes sellers do not want to alert their tenants to a potential sale. The idea that rents may be increased or leases not renewed can be very unsettling for both residential and commercial tenants. This could cause tenants to prematurely look for new locations, resulting in greater vacancies and a lower value for the owner's property.

Some service providers are substantially cheaper than others. But this is an area where you often "get what you pay for." There are clearly industry professionals that are reasonably priced, experienced, motivated, and very value adding. Just be sure not to sacrifice too much quality in return for a better price. The costs incurred by using the right industry professionals are minimal in comparison to the additional profits that they can help you generate from a wealth of knowledge and through risk mitigation.

Chapter 11

INVESTMENT STRATEGIES

The type of investment strategy employed by each individual will be based upon his personal objectives and risk tolerance levels. In addition, the current stage of a particular real estate market and the potential direction in which such market is heading will also be key considerations.

Chances are that the more aggressive your approach to real estate investing, the more risk you will be assuming. For example, if you want to buy many properties as soon as possible, you may be assuming large amounts of debt. With such a strategy, you want to ensure that you have adequate cash flow to cover the scheduled payments. In addition, the more properties that you own, the more potential vacancies and repair and maintenance costs.

Owning real estate over the long term has proven to be very profitable, especially due to the leverage that is usually associated with real estate investing. But property values have clearly performed substantially better or worse in certain periods than in others. As mentioned, no one can perfectly and intentionally time the market at exact peaks and troughs. But since real estate cycles usually move gradually and last for significant periods, having reasonable market timing can prove to be highly profitable.

Each investor will make his own decisions as circumstances arise and investment strategies can and often should change over time based upon current and evolving market conditions. I have seen the same investor employ different investment strategies for different properties all within the same market cycle. Each investment opportunity is unique.

There are several generic types of investment strategies that investors tend to utilize when investing in real estate.

BUY AND HOLD

As mentioned, real estate values have historically continued to increase over time. Of course, we know that the better the location, the greater the appreciation that we should expect. You never want to buy properties for the long term in areas with unfavorable demographics and low expected demand.

Buying and holding income-producing properties has its advantages. Just as with the stock markets, many people buy and sell real estate at the wrong time, which is often driven by greed and fear. Individual investors tend to buy high and sell low. There have been many studies performed proving that in general, investors are better off holding their stocks long term rather than trying to time the market. Many people have regretted buying or selling properties much too early or too late.

A buy-and-hold strategy avoids the taxation of gains resulting from the sale of a property. However, as discussed, you can roll any gain from one property sale into the purchase of another property and defer the payment of capital gains taxes by using a Section 1031 like-kind exchange. But you also have to meet certain time requirements and other parameters in order to qualify for this treatment.

Over time, as your property rises in value and your rental income increases, you can refinance with larger loans. This allows you to continue to take more equity out of the property, which can be used for additional property acquisitions. In addition, you will be reducing your loan balance over time through principal payments and normal amortization, which will also continue to increase your equity balance in the property.

TIMING THE MARKET

As can be seen by the severely depressed housing markets around most of the nation, markets can decline dramatically and for extended periods of time. Some analysts predict that it will take until 2012 or later before some housing markets return to 2003 or 2004 pricing levels. If you bought a Las Vegas residential property in the 1990s and continued to hold it, you would likely have experienced huge declines in value during the past few years. However, your property may have also had rapid appreciation for a five-year period. Under the buy-and-hold approach, your long-term appreciation may have been favorable and closer to historical averages when the entire period is considered.

But if you had bought a Las Vegas single-family home in late 2005 at the peak of the market and considered the value of your property in 2008, you would have most likely been disappointed. Under such a scenario, your property may have lost 30% or more of its value and be worth less than the amount of debt on the property. In addition, in today's market, your property would be competing with many others for tenants and it would most likely be many years before your investment became profitable.

This example supports the rationale behind attempting to time the market when buying and selling properties. While you probably will not time your decisions perfectly, getting reasonably close can result in substantial profits and protect you from downside risks. In addition, buying and selling properties allows investors to recycle their capital more quickly and participate in more transactions. For example, an investor may only have enough cash to purchase one property during a five-year period. But by employing a more active strategy, the same investor may acquire and sell many properties during the same time period and be able to generate substantially more profits.

While national markets tend to move more generally, when you are focusing on local markets, there are more micro events that can result in the rise and fall of real estate values more frequently. This is especially true when you are looking at specific sections and blocks within a particular city.

If you can buy properties in locations that are poised for rapid growth and increased demand, renovation or other type of value-adding event, your efforts can prove to be quite successful. The key is to know when to buy and when to sell. On one hand, you do not want to be buying at inflated prices after everyone else has purchased property with the same expectations. On the other hand, you do not want to buy too early and be holding a property in a stagnant market for 20 years before something favorable happens.

THE "DO NOTHING" QUICK FLIP

While trying to time the market can be a somewhat aggressive strategy, buying properties with the intent of quickly selling or "flipping" them for a profit can be an even bolder approach. Doing so requires a rapidly increasing market. This was the strategy of many novice investors during the recent residential housing run-up. Many people made significant profits buying houses and then selling them three to six months later. However, just like the game of musical chairs, those holding properties when the music stops are the losers.

Another way to buy and flip a residential property is by purchasing a new home before it is constructed. In such cases, you can usually place a small deposit on the commitment to buy a home once completed at some point in the future. Your hope is that shortly after the house is built, you can sell it for a substantially higher price. Under a perfect scenario, you can find a buyer before you actually take ownership of the home, thus avoiding obtaining formal financing and any associated carrying costs such as insurance, property taxes, and general mainte-nance. Strong demand is required for such a strategy to be successful since you are competing with home builders that may be selling hundreds or even thou-sands of similar homes.

PROPERTY IMPROVEMENT

A popular and sound method to buying and selling real estate is based upon improving a property's condition and corresponding value through renovation, upgrades, repairs or by altering or expanding its permitted uses. This approach places less reliance on market appreciation. Essentially, you are taking a distressed or unattractive property and turning it into something more desirable.

The property-improvement approach is a lower risk strategy when compared to alternatives that rely on market timing or rapid market appreciation. Improving a property's condition and appearance can be profitable in up, down, and flat markets. Often, unattractive and less-desirable properties are selling at substantial discounts due to the amount of effort and money involved in making the needed improvements.

Some risks associated with this approach include overspending to improve a property. I have seen some investors want to use the best materials, fixtures, and other upgrades so that finished property is of the highest quality. However, such improvements sometimes do not equate to a higher value. In such cases, either the targeted sales price is unreasonably high or the renovations cost substantially more than initially budgeted.

Many "handy" people have become successful real estate investors by performing many of the needed property repairs themselves. For example, a handyman I know buys a house in need of substantial improvement about every three to four years. He and his wife live in each house while he makes the needed repairs and alterations in his spare time. If a particular task falls outside of his expertise, he has plenty of industry contacts to call upon. The couple ultimately sells each house for a substantial profit before moving into the next one.

Increasing the cash flow that a property generates is another way to raise its value. As we will discuss further, if you can increase the occupancy rate of a property, raise rents, and better the tenant and lease quality, you can add substantial value and make great profits.

Altering a property's permitted use can also add substantial value under all market conditions. The craze a few years ago was converting apartment buildings into condominiums. While many investors are now defaulting on their bank loans and losing their properties due to insufficient sales volumes, millions of dollars were made on more successful projects. The projects that have experienced problems are clearly related to overpayment in an overheated market rather than the actual strategy of converting the apartments into condominiums.

Taking vacant land and working through the political zoning process can also substantially increase a property's value. I know numerous investors that focus only on buying raw land. They spend six to twelve months working with engineers and city officials to obtain a specific type of zoning for each property. Nothing can legally be built upon a vacant piece of land until the proper city approvals have been obtained. A real estate investor may work toward receiving the ultimate consent from a city to build a project such as a master planned residential community or an office park. Such a process can greatly enhance a property's value. Once the zoning process is complete, the investor may choose to sell the property, take profits, and allow someone else to handle the construction phase.

BUYING FORECLOSURE PROPERTY

A timely investment strategy entails the buying of property owned by banks and other lenders. These financial institutions lend money to homeowners and investors to purchase properties. If property owners cannot make their scheduled payments, lenders will declare their loans in default and take possession of the underlying real estate. Most lenders are in the business of making loans and not owning real estate, so their objective becomes selling their foreclosure properties quickly.

Sometimes lenders try to sell their residential properties in bulk sales. In such cases, you need to have substantial capital available to consider such purchases. When buying in bulk, you can usually negotiate a low purchase price, but you are also forced to take the "good with the bad" since you are usually not given the option of selecting specific properties.

Lenders will often engage local Realtors to sell residential and commercial foreclosure properties on an individual basis. At the time of this writing in late 2008, there are numerous residential foreclosure properties on the market and many more on the way. Many investors are getting tremendous bargains by buying these properties at substantial discounts at or near the bottom of a residential real estate market cycle.

Some foreclosure properties will be in better condition than others. When people realize that they will be losing their properties to a lender, they tend to be more careless and sometimes even intentionally destructive. Make sure you have a strong handle on required repair costs before considering such purchases.

"NO MONEY DOWN" PURCHASING

You see the advertisements on television for "no money down" real estate investing. In fact, some of these infomercials tell you that you can walk away with cash from sellers when buying their properties. Energetic salespeople sure make it look easy. Just buy their books or tapes or take their seminars and you can buy all of your property without having any cash and be filthy rich in no time!

It is possible to buy properties with no money down, but these opportunities are much fewer and farther in between than many people will lead you to believe. If you can do it, you can make huge profits. The key is to find desperate sellers that are willing to finance a portion of the purchase price for you. For example, assume a seller will take $100,000 for his property. Also assume that a bank will lend you $80,000 toward the purchase. If the seller agrees to lend you $20,000, you have effectively bought the property with no money down.

It is easier to find desperate sellers in down markets. Sellers with substantial equity in their properties can make good candidates to provide "seller financing" (also known as "carry back" financing). So do those that are looking for monthly income from your loan payments. It never hurts to ask when you are negotiating. Just remember that there is a fine line between savvy real estate investing and taking advantage of people that are down on their luck.

I do not encourage sellers to offer or agree to seller financing for two reasons. First of all, your loan to the buyer will be subordinate to the loan of a traditional lender. This means that if the buyer defaults on his loan to a bank, the bank will take the property and sell it. If the bank recovers its entire principal balance, past due interest, late fees, selling expenses, and any other costs associated with the foreclosure process, any remaining cash will go to you as a subordinate lender. But as we know, banks tend to sell foreclosure properties quickly and often at discounted prices. The chances of you getting paid a dime under such circumstances are slim. Alternatively, you may be able to assume the mortgage from the lender to better control the property, but you will then be obligated to make the scheduled payments and ultimately repay the debt. Secondly, to compensate you for providing such a risky loan, you should be charging the buyer a double-digit interest rate. Most seller financing terms are more generous to the buyer than the seller.

PASSIVE INVESTING

Each form of real estate investing will have its own levels of owner participation. Using a property management firm to manage your properties can significantly reduce your responsibilities and time commitments. Investors can also get exposure to real estate through more passive investments by pooling capital with other investors and allowing other people to manage one or more properties. Such investment ownership may range from only a few investors to tens of thousands of investors.

As discussed in an earlier chapter, investors can buy individual REIT stocks just as they would buy the stock of any other company. Specific investments can be selected based upon a specific REIT's investment strategy. For example, if you want to invest in hotels, you can buy the stock of a REIT that focuses on this sector of the market. For further diversification, there are mutual funds that focus solely on owning REIT stocks. These funds own hundreds of different companies that invest in numerous types of real estate. I am a firm believer in the benefits of diversification, and therefore, the majority of my REIT investments are held within REIT mutual funds.

Limited partnership (LP) and limited liability company (LLC) investments allow investors to finance projects being managed by real estate investors, developers, and other sponsors and participate in any profits. A simplistic example might be the buying and holding of a couple hundred acres of land for future appreciation. More complicated projects could include the construction of a hotel or residential community. Often, investors are asked to provide a certain amount of equity capital to seed the project. Then the sponsor will usually borrow additional funds from a bank or other lender. Assuming the project is profitable after repaying the lender and all of the project costs, some type of profit split is made between the investors and the sponsor.

When looking at such ventures with project sponsors, make sure that the ongoing fees paid to oversee the project are not excessive. For example, if the strategy is to buy and hold land, a minimal fee would be expected (if any). If overseeing a large construction project, a larger fee would make sense. I would also expect the investors in such projects to earn a minimum return before the sponsor sees any profits. For example, a transaction may be structured so that when a project is completed, the investors receive their original investment plus a 10–20% return before the sponsor receives any profits. After the investors are paid their minimum profits (often called a ''preferred return''), any remaining profits might be split 75% to the investors and 25% to the project sponsor.

There are many types of real estate investment funds that invest in various types of real estate. Each fund has its own strategy. For example, one may focus on buying distressed properties. Another may focus on real estate lending. Some may target properties in certain foreign countries. Such funds usually have targeted investment horizons ranging from three to seven years. The profits can be significant for such investments, but investors can often expect to have their capital tied up for the life of a fund. I would also expect similar investor profit-sharing structures for such funds as for LP and LLC investments.

Tenant in common (TIC) real estate ownership is a popular way for investors to participate in the ownership of a large property. A sponsor arranges for the purchase of one property by a group of TIC investors. For example, an entity might be formed to purchase and own a retail shopping center. The sponsor would find a number of investors to invest under a tenant in common structure and each investor would own a portion of the entity. The sponsor would earn a management fee each month for overseeing the investment and the investors would receive any distributions remaining after paying debt and property mainte-nance and repair costs.

TIC investments offer very limited liquidity to investors. In addition, they often have high sales commissions which reduce the profitability to investors. Also, owning one property does not offer the diversification benefits of owning multiple properties, such as through REIT ownership.

Another way to invest in real estate is by being a lender. Some real estate invest-ors purchase interests in loans to real estate developers. For example, a broker may find a real estate developer looking to borrow $10 million to construct an office building. The broker would try to raise the money for the developer by offering participation interests in the loan to numerous investors. The end result might be 50 to 100 investors each funding and owning a portion of a $10 million loan. The broker would earn a fee from the developer for arranging the loan and would often oversee the collection of payments from the borrower each month, which he would remit to the investors (less a small administrative or "servicing fee"). These loans (often called hard money loans) normally pay interest rates of 10–14% and have terms ranging from a few months to two years.

SUMMARY

The level of risk and the profitability potential can vary significantly depending upon your particular real estate investment strategy. Any strategy based on the expectation for rapid market appreciation has more risk than those that provide for the ability to hold properties longer term. This does not mean that you should not be opportunistic and buy and sell properties under the right circum-stances. However, having holding power and being able to own properties for longer periods of time results in a lower risk strategy. Those strategies that focus on property improvement can also encompass lower risk and often be highly profitable.

Many real estate funds and ventures are issued on a private placement basis, which means that under the guidelines of the Securities and Exchange

Commission (SEC), you may need to meet accreditation standards by having a minimum net worth or a minimum amount of annual income. These SEC guidelines are intended to protect unsophisticated investors. Private investments are often the most illiquid and provide investors with the least amount of information over the life of the investment. In addition, some are more speculative than others and fees paid to managers and sponsors may be more or less reasonable for each investment.

The level of required owner participation varies by investment strategy and should be a consideration. If a property management firm is hired to oversee the day-to-day responsibilities of direct property ownership, such costs should be considered when assessing a property's projected profitability. When allowing others to manage more passive investments, ensure that a strong track record and reputation exists. In addition, it would be prudent to have an experienced real estate attorney review any type of private placement prior to making an investment.

Chapter 12

CHARACTERISTICS OF UP, DOWN, AND FLAT MARKETS

No one can perfectly time a specific stage of a real estate market cycle and know exactly when to buy or sell to make the most money possible. If this is accomplished, it is done so through pure luck. However, there are many signs that investors can monitor to better assess the particular stage of a real estate market and help predict where the cycle is headed.

GREED AND FEAR

Wall Street often uses the term "greed and fear" to describe the motivations behind many stock, bond, and other securities investors. The interpretation of this statement is that the greed of investors pushes them to continue buying in a rising market because they are afraid of losing profit opportunities. This irrational behavior continues to push markets upward even when most logic does not support such high prices. Perfect examples include the technology boom that came to a screeching halt in the late 1990s and the unjustified run-up in residential housing prices during the early to mid-2000s.

After greed pushes markets to unjustified levels, people ultimately realize that such prices are not sustainable and they begin to panic. The stocks of start-up technology companies with no near to mid-term ability to generate earnings are not worth $100 a share. Housing prices cannot keep rising when most Americans cannot afford to buy a home. Upon such realizations, people begin to sell as quickly as possible. When others see a significant amount of sellers in an overpriced market, they too begin to panic. A snowballing effect takes place and before you know it, everyone is selling and markets are plummeting.

There is clearly such a mentality when it comes to real estate investing. Many people knew that the residential housing market was peaking in the mid-2000s. This included the investors that continued to speculatively buy residential real estate assuming that they could sell their properties before any market decline.

Overly optimistic others foolishly thought that this raging and overpriced market would have a "soft landing." Also fueling this upcoming debacle were countless lenders that continued to provide aggressive loans to home buyers and investors.

In the late 1990s and early 2000s, my wife was accumulating a portfolio of rental properties in Orlando, Florida. She would buy a couple properties each year, refinance existing properties, and oversee the property management aspects of residential real estate ownership.

Before making purchase decisions, my wife would ask my thoughts on the overall profit potential of a specific property. To make such an assessment, I would forecast the expected rent, available financing terms, and expenses for each property. I tried to keep my assumptions fairly conservative. I assumed a normal appreciation rate of 4–5% per year, an allowance for repairs and maintenance, insurance and property tax expense, etc.

I would enter all of the property assumptions into a model that I had created (you will be given instructions and access to this model toward the end of the book). Once the assumptions were entered, with the push of a button, the model told me what the expected average annual return would be for the property. I always targeted 12% per year or more.

In the late 1990s, it was easy to buy a property in Florida that could be rented and expected to generate an average annual return of 15% or more. In fact, we were buying three-bedroom houses for about $125,000 each and renting them for around $1,000 or more per month. But as each year passed, prices continued to rise and it became harder and harder to make the numbers work.

As my wife continued to look for more houses to purchase, the expected average annual return for most properties dropped below 12%, which was our limit. As the projected profitability kept declining due to continuously rising housing prices, we stopped buying, but continued to watch the market. We looked at other properties, but the average annual profits we were forecasting began to drop into the single digits. Some forecasted profits for specific properties were negative, meaning that the investment would have produced a loss.

It was sometime during the year 2003 that my wife and I decided that the residential real estate market was unrealistically high, that deals no longer made sense, and that the overall market needed to fall dramatically. So we decided to sell our entire portfolio of properties. We began negotiating with tenants to buy specific houses, we listed others for sale as leases matured, and we were eventually able to sell all of our properties before the market began its rapid decent.

I am grateful that we made the decision to sell. The Florida real estate market is now one of the worst in the country. Prices have fallen by over 25% and such declines are expected to continue. In addition, many forecasters expect that it will take many years to get back to peak 2005 and 2006 pricing levels. We did not time the market perfectly. In fact, after we had sold most of our properties, the market continued to rise. But we chose not to be overly greedy. Real estate is an illiquid asset and selling it takes time, even in good markets. I would still be kicking myself today if I had let greed win over rational thinking.

Greed pushes markets upward to unsupported price levels, which creates great selling opportunities. The trick is to not become too greedy and to consider selling when the signs of an overheated market are apparent. On the other hand, fear tends to push markets to unreasonably low pricing, which creates great buying opportunities. The goal here is to avoid "catching a falling knife" and to not purchase properties until market fundamentals make more sense. In addition, one of the benefits of real estate investing is that if you hold a property for a long enough period of time (the "buy-and-hold" strategy), chances are that you will earn attractive profits over the long term.

FOCUS ON LOCAL MARKETS

While most of the news you will see focuses on national real estate markets, real estate investors need to focus more on local and regional conditions. It is important to realize that the attractiveness and performance of one local real estate market can vary dramatically from another. Even markets that are within the same state and close to one another can experience significantly different growth rates and performance patterns.

While price appreciation in residential housing was dramatic during the early to mid-2000s across most of the United States, there were vast differences in appreciation rates depending upon each local market. For example, Las Vegas, Phoenix, and Miami all had home price increases of 100% or more over a five-year period, while most cities in Texas and Pennsylvania had slow or no growth.

We talked about factors that drive real estate values in an earlier chapter. It really boils down to supply and demand. While this is a very general statement and there are numerous factors that affect the desirability of a local market, the more demand and the less supply, the greater the values for real estate. It is good to stay abreast of national market conditions and economic news because national trends clearly have an impact on local markets. However, as a real estate investor, your specific focus should always be on the local conditions that are expected to affect your targeted property values.

As with all types of markets, many people have differing opinions. Some people think the stock market is going to rise dramatically, others think it will crash. People bet on opposite sides every day on numerous items such as oil and gold prices, foreign currencies, and water rights. You will also find many differing opinions regarding the future direction of a current real estate market. I find the most optimistic people are those that benefit from favorable market conditions. Most Realtors and even representatives of the National Association of Realtors usually overly stress the favorable points of any market cycle and downplay any negatives. The better the markets, the more money these people earn.

Knowledge is an asset and I am a firm believer in learning as much as possible about a relevant subject. But be skeptical and come to your own conclusions. Everyone has an opinion and many of them will prove to be wrong. No one can predict the future, but the more educated the forecaster, the higher the probability of accuracy.

RESIDENTIAL MARKETS

There are many variables that can indicate whether residential real estate markets are up, down, or flat. In addition, recent trends in such data can provide an indication of where markets are heading. My wife and I came to the conclusion that the Florida residential housing market was extremely overvalued by monitoring some of the information below.

1. Annual Appreciation—Typically, a strong, upward market is characterized by abnormal annual appreciation rates in home values. Remember that property values move differently in different markets based upon supply and demand. I do not want to suggest that you should immediately sell your properties in years in which property values are rapidly increasing. In fact, these should be your most profitable years. Abnormal appreciation may be the result of a rebound from a severe downturn or higher demand that is justified by economic growth.

   When assessing whether a market is too overvalued and set for an ultimate decline, you need to look at many other factors in totality. But do consider appreciation trends. If housing prices have risen dramatically for several years, this may be a red flag.

   The national appreciation rate for single-family homes has averaged about 3–5% historically, but again, these numbers vary significantly by region and city. In a weak market, you can expect growth rates to be lower than this range. In down markets, you can expect declines in prices. The severity and duration of each market cycle will vary depending upon specific circumstances.

2. Forecasted Profitability—When buying single-family houses and condominiums no longer generates acceptable forecasted profits under reasonable assumptions, this can be a strong indication of an overheated market that needs a correction. In such cases, we tend to be sellers rather than buyers.

   When I buy real estate, I normally assume a holding period of at least five years for modeling purposes. I may sell a property sooner or never sell the property at all. But to forecast profitability, I must assume a sale at some point in the future. Since buying and selling real estate often includes significant transaction costs and since real estate is usually an illiquid asset, it often takes a while for a property to increase in value.

   With this book, you will be provided instructions for using a Real Estate Acquisitions Model that is posted on my Web site. This is essentially the same model that I used to assist my wife when acquiring single-family homes in Florida.

   When the forecasted profitability of most properties continues to drop, I view this as a strong warning sign that property values may be getting overheated. Profitability declines within the model when monthly rents are not increasing at a fast enough pace to support rising property values.

3. Cash Flow—Another quantitative factor I consider when looking at residential properties is the assumed level of monthly cash that a property generates. The model I provided considers this factor in its calculations. When rented properties are expected to generate strong cash flow each month after considering average repair costs, taxes and insurance, mortgage payments, and any other cash outflows, this often suggests that properties are fairly priced or even underpriced.

   When there is no additional expected cash (or negative cash flow) at the end of each month based on current rents, interest rates, and expenses, this can often be a sign that property values are getting too high. But the expected cash flow can vary based upon the amount of leverage employed and the type of loan chosen, so cash flow cannot be a telling factor on its own. But the model considers all of the relevant quantitative factors when computing the expected average annual return for a property.

4. Inventory—The current number of homes for sale in a given area can be a telling figure when assessing the present and future state of a residential housing market. The average number of homes for sale in a local market is compared to the current monthly sales rate of homes in the same area. For example, if there are 5,000 homes for sale and sales are taking place at a rate of 1,000 homes per month, there is five months of housing inventory on the market. Based on these figures, it is expected to take approximately five months to sell all the houses currently available for sale. Five to six months of home inventory would be an indication of a normal market.

   In strong residential real estate markets, you would expect to see home inventories substantially lower. In a weak market, home inventories are much higher. For example, during the year 2008, residential home inventories across the nation averaged between ten and twelve months. Again, too much supply and not enough demand. The abundant number of home foreclosures is increasing supply and many buyers are sitting on the sidelines based on economic worries or the anticipation that home prices will fall further.

5. Time on the Market—In a normal market, you might expect a residential property to take several months to sell. As discussed, real estate transactions take time. There is a lot of work required to facilitate a change in ownership. In addition, buying a home is usually a very personal decision. People take their time and look at many homes before making a purchase. In addition, most home viewings are done on weekends which tend to extend the process.

   When markets start declining, it takes longer to sell homes and the average time that houses remain on the market begins to increase. Under normal conditions, you might expect an average selling time period of three to five months. Stronger markets can result in substantially less time, while weaker markets can result in substantially longer times to sell properties.

   This average number of days that a home spends on the market is definitely a trend worth watching closely. Business news media often report this information each month. As the average number of days on the market begins to increase, a market may be heading for a downturn. As this figure decreases, a market may be poised for above-normal appreciation.

6. Affordability—A housing affordability index is a measurement tool that indicates the percentage of homeowners or first-time home buyers that can afford the median-priced home in a given city, state, or region of the country. As the percentage rises, more people can afford to buy homes. As the percentage declines, less people can afford to buy homes.

   As you can imagine, when more people can afford to buy houses, home prices are more reasonably priced and prices have a greater chance of increasing. However, as housing prices continue to rise and more and more people can no longer afford to buy, the chances become greater that prices should decline (or not rise or rise as quickly).

   A housing affordability index is generally computed based upon the average price of a starter home in an identified area (national, regional, or local), the average amount of household income, and the current level of interest rates for home mortgages. If interest rates or home prices rise, the index declines and fewer people can afford homes. If incomes rise and interest rates and home prices remain stable, then more people can afford to purchase homes. Usually local and national realty associations will compute this number on a monthly basis. Such patterns should be monitored over time.

Another trend to consider is that when housing is less affordable, more people are renting. Depending upon the supply of rental units in the market (apartments, condos, and single-family homes), lower housing affordability can result in higher rental rates. However, the value of individual residential properties is usually less affected by how much income a property can generate than when compared to commercial properties. Particularly when transitioning between market cycles, you may be getting higher rents and better cash flow when housing affordability is low, but less appreciation in general housing prices due to lower demand from home buyers seeking new residences.

7. Rent-to-Value—When considering long-term trends, home prices have historically averaged less than 15 times annual rents. For example, based upon such an approach, a single-family home that can be rented for $1,500 a month would be valued at approximately $270,000 (15 times annual rent of $18,000). As the residential housing markets continued to overheat in the early to mid-2000s, this multiple rose substantially. For example, housing in Florida, Arizona, and California reached multiples of 20 times or greater. This means that a house valued at $500,000 that can be rented for $25,000 a year ($2,083 per month) is really only worth about $375,000 ($25,000 times 15) using such a historical multiple approach. While not an absolute or sole valuation methodology, rent-to-value multiples are another factor to consider when assessing a particular property.

8. The Cost to Construct—As I watch the current downturn in the residential housing market, many of the most overheated markets have experienced sales declines of over 25% and no one can say that the bottom has been reached. However, one indication to me that the bottom is near and that prices should start to rebound is the fact that many new houses are currently selling at prices that are substantially below the costs required to construct a new home.

Some construction costs will decline during market downturns, such as labor and certain materials when there is little building activity (i.e., lower demands leads to lower costs). However, when the costs to construct a new home are substantially higher than the selling prices of new homes, this can be an indication that home prices will be heading upward.

9. Housing Permits—The number of housing permit applications filed in a specific period can be an indication of future home construction. The number of housing permits requested has declined dramatically since the mid-2000 housing bust began. For example, in Orange County, California, one of the hardest hit areas, building permits reached a 52-year low during the year 2007.

Lower housing permits means lower construction and fewer new homes coming on the market. Over time, this can assist in lowering the supply of homes (although only about 15% of total home sales are from new homes versus existing homes).

10. Mortgage Delinquencies—A factor that many people are watching today is the number of homeowners that are delinquent in the payments of their mortgage loans. Current loan delinquencies are a strong indicator of upcoming property foreclosures. The more properties foreclosed upon and owned by banks and other lenders, the more properties that will ultimately be on the market for sale. As mentioned, lenders tend to sell properties fairly quickly and cheaply, which generally brings down the value of residential markets.

COMMERCIAL REAL ESTATE

Many of the same factors affecting residential real estate can affect commercial real estate values and trends. Supply and demand is still very applicable. As with any product, the more demand and less supply, the greater pricing power and the more prices should rise.

As the events of the year 2008 unfold, the residential housing markets are the worst they have been in many decades. In addition, there are signs of strain appearing on the commercial real estate markets as well. Just in Reno, Nevada, I have recently seen three restaurants, a doughnut shop, and several retail stores go out of business during a six-month period and all within a two-mile radius. With energy and food prices skyrocketing, home prices declining, and overall uncertainty about the economy, consumers are spending less. This has a direct impact on product and service sales and the demand for commercial space.

Consumer spending accounts for about two-thirds of the U.S. economy. When people slow their spending, employers need fewer employees to handle lesser consumer demand. In addition, profitability declines and employers are often forced to reduce work staffs in order to cut costs. This results in more unemployment and even less spending. This also leads to lower demand from businesses for commercial real estate.

Certain variables that reflect upward or downward pricing trends in residential real estate markets can also provide similar indications for commercial real estate markets. For example, if commercial markets have experienced several years of aggressive appreciation and demand is not keeping pace, this can be an indication of an overpriced market. Overpriced markets lead to lower cash flow and expected profitability when reasonable assumptions are used. Such variables can also reflect buying opportunities when forecasted cash flow and profitability are high.

Besides watching national and local economic activities, below are some additional benchmarks that I watch when assessing the direction of commercial real estate markets.

1. Capitalization Rates—We talked about how income-producing (properties leased to one or more tenants) commercial properties are usually valued using some type of income approach. The exact method varies depending upon the size, type, and complexity of a specific property. A capitalization rate, or "cap rate," is often determined by dividing the NOI of a property by its sales price.

    The higher the cap rate, the cheaper the property and vice versa. In booming markets, cap rates tend to be low, and in depressed markets, cap rates tend to be much higher. The general level of cap rates is also dependent upon the level of market interest rates. Higher interest rates lead to higher cap rates because the expected profitability of real estate is compared to the profitability of other investments. For example, if 10-year government bonds are paying investors 4%, cap rates on commercial properties may be 6%. When interest rates rise and the same 10-year bond is paying 6%, cap rates may be closer to 8%.

    Cap rates have been gradually rising in many markets as commercial properties have been in less demand. Cap rates vary by property type, lease terms, and tenant quality. Therefore, you cannot assume that a stand-alone restaurant property will sell at the same cap rate as a large shopping center. Nor will a property leased to a strong tenant be priced as high as a comparable property leased to a much weaker tenant. Because of such differences and because cap rates are often so correlated with general interest rates, it is difficult to provide estimated ranges under differing market cycles. But generally, if cap rates are between 5% and 7% in a strong market, they might be in the low double digits during a depressed market.

Depending on a specific property, one or more income approaches may be more or less appropriate. In rising markets, gross rent multipliers are increasing and NOI cap rates are declining. In addition, the discount rates used for discounted cash flow analyses get lower. In declining markets, gross rent multipliers are decreasing and NOI cap rates and discount rates are increasing.

2. Occupancy Rates—When you value commercial real estate based on an income approach, the more income a property is generating, the greater its value. Therefore, the greater the occupancy rate, the more rent being collected and the higher a property's value.

When demand for commercial space is low, occupancy rates and values decline. This is a trend that is taking place right now. In order to purchase a commercial property in today's market, I either expect a significant discount or will just wait until values fall further and I feel the bottom is near.

I know several real estate investors that focus solely on properties with low occupancy rates. They purchase these properties with the intent of increasing NOI by renovating the buildings and finding new and additional tenants. Once accomplished, they sell the properties based upon the higher amount of income and earn substantial profits.

3. Lease Rates—As you might expect, when demand for commercial property is low, more space is generally available for rent and greater competition exists among property owners. In such cases, owners are forced to lower rents in order to attract tenants. Sometimes, it takes time to see the effects of lower trending lease rates because existing leases need to mature before new rental rates can be negotiated by tenants.

Lease rates are strongly correlated with occupancy rates. When there is limited space in a specific market, then rents should be high. When there is excess space in a market and occupancy rates are low, then lease rates tend to be lower. Trending increases in lease rates will lead to higher property values, while declining lease rates will lead to lower property values.

When considering the purchase of commercial properties, evaluate and consider the features of any existing leases in place versus current market terms. For example, if a $500,000 property was purchased and leased to a tenant using a 10% lease rate, the annual rent would be $50,000. If the lease is near expiration and current lease rates for similar properties are only 7%, the property should only be expected to generate annual rent of $35,000. Therefore, the property should be valued assuming the lower market lease rate and its value will be lower than if the 10% lease rate had been assumed. Commercial real estate is valued based upon its future income or appreciation potential.

4. The General Economy—In a strong economy, consumers feel wealthier and spend more. Such environments result in lower unemployment and greater demand for products and services. Higher consumer demand leads to business growth. Greater demand from businesses leads to greater demand for commercial space and higher property values.

While local economic activity is most relevant to specific properties and investments, the state of the national economy often filters down to the regional and local levels. For example, if the government believes that the national economy is overheating, it will begin to raise interest rates, which will have slowdown effects on most of the nation. As with any type of investing, continue to monitor local, regional, and national economic conditions for directional signals.

5. Residential Housing Markets—As discussed, the demand for commercial real estate often follows the demand for residential housing. If housing growth has slowed in a particular area, there will be less demand for commercial property in the same and adjacent areas. Be careful when considering commercial properties that are surrounded by undeveloped land and numerous homes that are struggling to be sold. Such circumstances can lead to stagnant or declining commercial property values. The inverse is true when there is heavy residential activity. Under such circumstances, the demand for various types of commercial properties can increase dramatically.

SUMMARY

No individual statistic is enough to gauge a current real estate market or where such market is heading. And while making such assessments are subjective and somewhat more of an "art than science," spending time reviewing such information can provide good indications of where a market is ultimately heading. Again, no one can time a market peak or decline perfectly, but getting close can be very rewarding.

As with any type of investing, try not to let greed or fear control your decisions. The better business people make their choices based upon facts and not emotions. Do not always follow the crowd and be skeptical of the advice of others. Everyone has an opinion and opinions vary widely. The prudent investor comes to his own conclusions based upon supporting evidence.

Chapter 13

RESIDENTIAL REAL ESTATE INVESTING

A LOGICAL PROGRESSION

Investing in residential real estate includes the purchase and ownership of single-family homes, condominiums, duplexes, triplexes, and small apartment buildings consisting of four units or fewer. Residential structures of larger scale are considered to be commercial properties due to the additional complexities associated with such investments.

One of the simplest and most affordable ways that investors can own residential real estate is through the purchase of single-family homes. Many investors understand how the cash inflows and outflows work from such investments because they have had similar experiences through the ownership or renting of their own homes.

Owning single-family residential investment property is a significant accomplishment. For someone with no real estate investing experience, this is the first logical step toward direct property ownership.

There is only so much that can be taught by reading books and other publications. The most relevant experience is best learned by doing. Going through the process of visiting properties, negotiating prices, obtaining financing, reading leases, and seeing the revenues and expenses associated with property ownership provides investors with a wealth of knowledge. As with anything done for the first time, there will be ongoing lessons to be learned. The more experience you gain, the better you will become at real estate investing. Learn as much as you can from industry professionals and do not be afraid to ask questions.

After buying and renting your first property, you will see ways to improve the process going forward. Maybe with your next tenant, you will include landscaping and minimum repair bills as a tenant obligation in the lease. Maybe you will choose a different type of financing or use a different lender if you refinance or purchase another property. Your negotiation skills will sharpen each time you bid on or sell a property. Your network of professionals and service providers will continue to expand. You will start to pick up and use more industry terminology and have greater confidence. Over time, you will continue to learn and become a better and better real estate investor.

There is little difference between owning single-family homes and owning duplexes, triplexes, and other small residential properties. There will be two or more leases and rental streams and multiple tenants to manage. Some of the costs will be higher since such properties support multiple kitchens, separate heating and air conditioning systems, and perhaps more people wearing on the property. But after owning single-family homes, these types of properties should not require a significant increase in expertise.

There is always the challenge of finding the money to purchase one or more properties. I realize that producing down payments of tens of thousands of dollars for each property is difficult for most people. But it normally takes a long time to build a substantial portfolio of real estate investments. People tend to save money from other sources, borrow against their primary residences or other collateral, work with sellers to obtain carry back financing, seek lenders willing to lend greater dollar amounts, etc. Each investor's ultimate success in raising such capital is contingent on market conditions and individual circumstances. Just remember not to take on more leverage than you can handle.

Your personal investment strategy might include buying one property, holding it for a number of years, and then selling it. Assuming that your property is increasing in value and that you are paying your loan balance down over time, after selling the property you should have a substantially greater amount of cash remaining than when you started. Now you can buy a larger property or perhaps two smaller properties. Building wealth is a long-term process.

As properties appreciate in value, they can eventually be refinanced with larger loan amounts so that excess cash can be taken and used to help purchase additional properties. For example, assume that you purchased a property for $150,000 using a loan from a bank based on an 80% LTV ratio. This means that you invested $30,000 of your own money and borrowed $120,000. If this property increases in value to $180,000, you can now refinance and borrow $144,000 (assuming 80% times $180,000). With this new loan, you can pay off your existing loan and still have an extra $24,000 in cash.

CHOOSING A PROPERTY

The attractiveness of a property can vary depending upon its location, condition, and overall characteristics. Depending upon your investment strategy, you may be planning to rent your property. In addition, at some point in the future, you will probably want to sell or refinance this asset as well.

A residential property's value is usually determined by the level of demand from home buyers and investors (substantially more so by home buyers). If you buy a property that is unappealing to potential tenants and buyers, then the appreciation of this property will most likely lag any appreciation in the general market.

Avoid properties having unique characteristics that make them less functional or unattractive unless part of your investment strategy is to correct such flaws.

Consider low ceilings, outdated architecture, dangerous locations, poor school districts, and other factors when looking at properties to acquire. Ask yourself what type of tenant you are targeting. Would you want to live in the home? Why or why not? What if your circumstances were different (i.e., if you did or did not have children, etc.)? What would you change about the property to make it more livable? How much would such improvements cost and would such expenditures result in a reasonably higher property value?

Your investment strategy may be to buy one or more run-down properties in poor areas. Maybe your property will serve as low-income housing or a dormitory for college students. In such cases, you probably do not want to invest a lot of money into these homes. Rather, you are relying on a relatively low investment to offset lower expected rents. If such investments are relying on significant appreciation over time, there needs to be compelling reasons why future demand for such properties will be strong.

Below are some generic guidelines that I have found helpful when investing in residential real estate.

- Consider multi-bedroom properties in good neighborhoods that will attract families who will often rent for extended periods of time. Tenant turnover costs can be expensive.
- Purchase generic properties without luxury features that can cause additional expense and liability (i.e., swimming pools, fancy equipment and fixtures, etc.).
- Avoid poor locations (like next to highways) and floor plans, garage conversions, and other features that could make a home less desirable for sale or rent.
- Have one or more professional inspections performed on the home before purchase and obtain estimates for any significant needed repairs.
- Get at least two quotes on financing alternatives and at least two estimates on all material repair work. I have seen huge differences between service providers.
- Obtain credit reports on any prospective tenants. I recommend requiring the first and last month's rent and a security deposit equal to one month's rent to cover any damages to the property.
- Forecast income and expenses and be comfortable that you can manage the payments when the property is occupied and vacant for significant periods of time.
- Do not base your total investment strategy on the expectation of abnormal, rapid price increases.
- Forecast your expected average annual return for a specific holding period and make sure that the numbers make sense. Many investment properties are purchased without rational investment strategies.

FORECASTING PROFITABILITY

When considering the purchase of an investment property, whether it is for residential or commercial purposes, I always prepare a forecast of the expected average annual return that will be generated from the investment using fairly conservative assumptions. Doing so helps to ensure that I am making a prudent investment that is expected to make money. But it also aids in determining an appropriate price to offer a seller.

When computing a potential bid for a particular piece of residential property, I tend to base my offer on both comparable market prices for similar properties and a purchase price that allows me to earn an acceptable level of profit. Many times, current market prices do not allow me to earn my minimum targeted return and I choose not to buy.

Enclosed in the Appendix are the instructions and a Web site address to access a profitability forecasting tool that my wife and I used when evaluating single-family real estate transactions. This model is simplistic and should be considered as being one of many tools and perspectives utilized when evaluating a particular piece of property. However, it should give you an idea of how many investors look at real estate profitability before making investments.

Because of the limited liquidity and high transaction costs associated with buying and selling real estate, I assume a minimum holding period of five years when preparing my profitability estimates. In reality, I may sell the property sooner or later depending on future circumstances and investment goals. But for forecasting purposes, I must assume a sales date and five years is a reasonable assumption. I also try to assume fairly conservative revenue, expense, and appreciation assumptions.

The average annual appreciation rate is one of the most important assumptions when forecasting the profitability of an investment. Rather than like some investors who assume their property values will increase by 10% or more per year, I tend to be more conservative. Since the national historical averages of residential home appreciation tend to be between 3% and 5% a year, my annual appreciation assumptions are usually not outside of this range. I hope that I am being conservative and that my investment will appreciate more rapidly based upon the purchase price and the growth potential, but I want to make sure that I meet my minimum profitability threshold under conservative assumptions.

One of the first things I look at when assessing a particular piece of property and when considering a potential bidding price is the available financing package. I always ask my mortgage brokers and lenders for different financing options so that I can compare each one in the model. For example, I may be offered a loan package with an 80% loan-to-value limit at a certain interest rate. Another financing alternative might include a 90% loan-to-value package with a higher interest rate.

An additional benefit of including the model is to allow investors to see the effects of leverage first hand. See what happens to the projected profitability when you adjust the loan-to-value ratio up and down. You will find that the use of leverage is a key component to the profitability of real estate investing (assuming it is a reasonably profitable investment).

I usually choose a 30-year, fixed rate loan. Some people tend to choose fixed rate loans with shorter maturities (i.e., 15 years) depending upon their specific investment objectives. You will often find in the model that longer term loans (assuming longer principal amortization schedules) result in higher expected returns. This concept ties back to the benefits of leverage. If leverage helps increase my expected returns, why would I want to repay it sooner with a shorter amortization schedule? In addition, with longer term loans, you can lock in your borrowing costs for greater periods. If interest rates rise over time, your cost of borrowing will not change during the term of the loan. If interest rates decline over time, you can refinance the loan.

Many people choose variable rate loans with payments that change over time. But I am not in the business of determining where interest rates are heading. Most economists are unsuccessful in forecasting mid- to long-term interest rates and doing so is a primary function of their jobs. If they cannot do so consistently, there is no reason to think that I can.

Many investors choose shorter term loans to benefit from lower interest rates or no initial amortization. Both factors can be beneficial, particularly for investors with predetermined investment horizons. But when I buy a property, I often do not know when I will be selling the asset. It may be in five years, ten years, or never. And I certainly do not have any intention of selling a property during an unfavorable real estate market. Rather, if I decide to sell, I plan to maintain holding power when needed and sell under favorable market conditions. If I expect the property to continue increasing in value, I may never sell it and defer paying capital gains taxes on my profit.

If I do hold a property long term, I will most likely refinance my initial loan one or more times to take advantage of lower interest rates, higher rents, any increased value, and the general ability to obtain higher leverage. However, I do not know when that will be or how interest rates or real estate markets will behave in the meantime. This is part of my rational for long-term, fixed rate loans. But each investor has his own objectives and must choose which form of financing is most attractive.

Any property management costs need to be factored into the profitability of a particular property. Paying up to 10% of rental income to a property management firm has a significant bearing on the profitability of an investment. There are many benefits that an experienced property manager can provide. Each investor will need to weigh the costs and benefits when deciding whether to employ a property management firm.

Property management companies will know the appropriate rental rates for their active markets and for specific properties in these areas. Other sources for comparable rents in a targeted area include local newspapers and the Internet. Estimating accurate rental rates for a potential property prior to purchase will have a significant effect on its overall profitability. For example, if you assume that you can rent a property for $2,000 a month and after purchase you realize that the property is only worth $1,500 a month, your average annual expected return will decline dramatically. In such cases, what appeared to be a great investment may turn out to be regretful.

A significant cost related to a rental property can be vacancy time. There are times when there is no rent being generated from a property, yet as owner you are still obligated to pay the mortgage, power and water bills, and any maintenance expenses. Such costs need to be estimated when forecasting your average annual expected return.

As tenants move in and out, there are associated costs. Some of these expenses can be deducted from the prior tenant's security deposit. Other costs are just part of the normal wear and tear on the property. Any expected owner costs should be considered as part of the average monthly expenses when forecasting the profitability of an investment.

Before purchasing a property, my wife and I would either have the seller repair all material items, discount the purchase price, or have the contract provide for some type of monetary allowance. The big expenses that need to be taken care of either immediately or at some point in the future usually pertain to items such as the roof, heating and air conditioning system, carpeting, and paint. But depending on the condition of the home, we sometimes had to repair electrical panels, replumb, remove trees too close to the foundation, retile bathrooms, etc. The key is having a good cost estimate and including it in your forecast as an up-front expense.

Since our leases required the tenants to cut the grass, maintain the landscaping, and pay their own utility bills, the primary costs that I worried about were any up-front expenses required to get the property ready for rent and the ongoing repair costs.

Real estate taxes are another significant cost. The current real estate taxes should be disclosed by sellers and show up on MLS listings. Beware of potential tax increases that can take place after you purchase a property. For example, chances are that you are buying the property at a higher price than the seller paid. In such cases, the new sales price could trigger the taxing authorities to increase the tax assessment based on the increased value. In addition, sometimes specific states give real estate tax reductions when a property is serving as the owner's primary residence. If you are planning to rent the property, such tax concessions no longer apply and the tax bill will increase. Tax bills associated with specific pieces of property can periodically increase based on state policies and valuation methods as well.

You will also need to estimate the initial insurance costs associated with owning a rental property. Also, as your property increases in value, you may want to increase your insurance coverage, which will add to this cost in the future. In addition, insurance rates often tend to rise over time. Sometimes these increases can be substantial based upon certain events (i.e., hurricanes, earthquakes, etc.). An insurance agent can provide you with an initial estimate before you purchase a property.

Many properties are in communities that require monthly or annual fees (i.e., homeowners' associations). It is worthwhile to ask for information showing historical price increases and if there were ever any special fee assessments. I have seen some communities that are less desirable because they were never set up properly by the builder and homeowners have been forced to make unexpected payments.

When assuming the sale of a property, there will be selling expenses. These costs can include cleaning, painting, real estate commissions, and other costs. Not knowing the condition of the property in the future, I usually just assume most of these costs to be a percentage of the sales price. Remember that as a seller using the services of a real estate agent, you normally pay the commissions of the buyer's real estate agent and your real estate agent.

After speaking so much about rent and the various costs that can be associated with a particular property, perhaps it is best to begin inputting assumptions into the model and seeing the results. As noted, this tool is fairly simplistic and is not intended to serve the needs of every investor or assess the profitability of every property. However, investors should be able to effectively use this tool when evaluating most residential property acquisitions. Please be sure to read the instructions in the Appendix.

My primary purpose for providing the model is to show investors the need for an investment strategy when acquiring real estate. I have watched too many people acquire properties in recent years expecting the price to surge and the property to be sold in three to six months for a large profit. Unfortunately, for many people this strategy never materialized and they have been stuck with high-cost properties, an unfavorable real estate market, and rental rates that cannot even come close to their monthly mortgage payments.

I have never seen anyone in the business world buy or lend against a residential or commercial property without computing some type of value and profitability estimate. The model I provide is one way to estimate the profitability of a particular property assuming a five-year holding period. This is a reasonable way to assess a property's potential under a buy-and-hold strategy. Even if you plan to hold a property for ten years or longer, if the first five years do not indicate a reasonably profitable investment, maybe you should not be buying the property.

The model provided is not a useful tool when seeking a more aggressive and active strategy such as when attempting to time the market or when planning to buy, improve, and then quickly sell a property. However, the model can still be a useful resource under such scenarios. It is always helpful to know that if your primary strategy does not unfold as planned, a longer term hold will still result in a profitable investment (or one that minimizes losses).

SUMMARY

Purchasing residential properties is an easy way for investors to begin directly owning real estate. The business model associated with owning residential properties for investment purposes is fairly straightforward and most people can understand the cash inflows and outflows based upon personal experience.

Depending upon your investment strategy and the current market cycle, buying residential real estate may be more or less advantageous. Sometimes it is best to sit on the sidelines and wait for better buying opportunities. In such cases, it may be a good time to sell. Other times, buying opportunities are abundant.

The key to successful real estate investing is to have a rational investment strategy. In addition, investors should study and understand current and expected market conditions and choose investments that are expected to earn sufficient profits under reasonable assumptions.

Chapter 14

RESIDENTIAL REAL ESTATE INVESTING: CASE STUDIES

CASE STUDY I

Investor:	John Stanley
Occupation:	Middle school teacher
Real estate experience:	Owner of three single-family rental homes in Orlando, Florida acquired over prior five years; currently looking to acquire fourth property
Property management:	Self-managed
Primary investment strategy:	Buy-and-hold
Current market conditions:	Up market with normal to strong appreciation expected to continue

Overview

John is very interested in real estate investing. He feels comfortable investing in residential real estate. John enjoys being actively involved and chooses to manage his own properties. John purchased his first property about five years ago. Two years later, he bought his second and then last year purchased his third property. Based on steady housing appreciation and increasing rents during the past five years, John can now refinance his first property with a larger loan and use the additional proceeds to purchase a fourth property.

Market Assessment

The general housing markets in Orlando are stable with normal to strong appreciation expected. The specific neighborhoods that John has targeted for his property ownership are in the suburbs about 15 miles outside of the downtown area. John sees favorable trends for this area and a strong rental market. John continues to stay abreast of relevant market information pertaining to the

Southeast, the city of Orlando, and the specific suburbs where his properties reside. John has considered the following factors when deciding to buy an additional property:

- People continue to move to the Southeast and specifically Orlando due to the favorable climate and the availability of diversified employment opportunities.
- The annual appreciation rate for housing has been about 5–7% per year for the past five years.
- There is currently about 4.5 months of housing inventory in the Orlando market based on recent sales figures.
- Properties currently remain on the market for an average of 130 days.
- While home prices are strong, Orlando remains affordable to a substantial number of home buyers.
- Interest rates are relatively low, mortgage delinquencies are low, and the general economy appears sound with relatively low unemployment.

The Team

John has established a relationship with a local Realtor. She was highly recommended by a neighbor and a business associate. The Realtor prints local property listings for John so that he can choose specific houses to visit. Once selected, the Realtor makes appointments and meets John at each property. She also provides great market insights when discussing specific properties and neighborhoods. The Realtor points out migration patterns, school districts, recent sales, and other relevant information. She sometimes has helpful facts about particular sellers based upon conversations with their Realtors and she aids in discussing potential negotiation tactics.

The same lender has arranged the financing for two of John's three existing properties. John feels comfortable with his relationship manager and feels like he seeks the best terms for John. John has referred friends and colleagues to the lender and the lender realizes the future business opportunities that John can provide. The same relationship manager is assisting John in refinancing one of his existing properties so that he can use the additional proceeds to help purchase his next property. John has also received quoted terms from a local mortgage broker.

John meets with his personal tax advisor each year and discusses his investment strategies. John has already been told that because he actively manages his properties, he can take all of the expected tax losses generated due to significant maintenance, repair, interest, and depreciation expenses. John's tax advisor has already discussed the requirements of a 1031 exchange with John in case he considers selling one or more properties. By doing so, John can avoid current capital gains tax payments.

John has a local insurance agent that is currently insuring all of his properties. The agent is very familiar with the markets where John invests and she is able to provide quick and accurate quotes when needed. John has compared quotes among several providers and has concluded that his current insurer is very competitive.

Due to his ownership of three existing properties, John has a list of dependable maintenance and repair firms. While he always relies on referrals when selecting a service provider, the first handyman John employed proved to be a disappointment. John later found someone more reliable and inexpensive.

John feels comfortable reviewing and negotiating his own documents when purchasing properties and entering leases with tenants. However, he did have an experienced real estate attorney review his initial lease to ensure that it was compliant with all state regulations and that it properly protected him as a landlord. John has the same attorney review his leases every two or three years to confirm that they remain compliant and secure. If John is ever forced to evict a tenant, he feels comfortable using the same attorney to represent him for such services.

Target Market

John has continued to target properties within a five-mile radius of his home. This close proximity allows him to visit properties easily when needed. The communities John is targeting consist mostly of three- and four-bedroom homes on roughly quarter-acre lots. Many are on cul-de-sacs. The neighborhoods have wide sidewalks and an abundance of trees. The homes are primarily block-style, single-floor and average about 1,600 square feet. There is plenty of relatively new retail shopping and restaurants in the area. Overall, the neighborhoods provide desirable housing and an attractive community.

Property Selection/Valuation/Projected Profitability

John performed the following steps before considering making offers to acquire his fourth property:

1. Based on his prior experience and current investment strategy, John continues to target single-family homes with three or more bedrooms in attractive neighborhoods that will appeal to tenants. John realizes that the longer the tenants stay, the more profitable his investment. Lower tenant turnover results in less property management and lower re-tenanting costs.
2. John looks for fairly generic homes without any special features that would result in additional costs like higher repair bills, greater insurance fees, etc. He purposely excludes homes with swimming pools.
3. John also avoids houses that have odd floor plans, garage conversions, or that are located on busy roadways or have close proximity to highways. He realizes that many properties with unique characteristics can be more difficult to rent and to sell. He also considers aspects of each neighborhood such as the quality of the school district.
4. John is aware of recent sales trends in his targeted area. His Realtor provided a list of homes that have recently been sold, the square footage and relevant features of each home, and the sales price per square foot.
5. Based on MLS listing summaries provided by his Realtor, John begins screening about a dozen houses for sale based upon type of home, location, and the asking price per square foot. After narrowing the list down to six, John drives by each property to better assess its curb appeal and other externally visible characteristics. Based on doing so, John narrows his top choices down to four houses.

6. John has received estimated interest rates and other lending terms from two lenders. He also has a letter from one of the lenders stating that he is preapproved for financing up to $190,000.
7. John forecasts the profitability of each property at full price to gain a better understanding of each opportunity. Any reduction in price will increase his average annual expected return.

    a. When forecasting profitability, John assumes an average annual appreciation rate of 4%. He believes that based on the strong demand for housing in his targeted areas that actual appreciation will be higher. However, he wants to remain conservative with his assumptions.
    b. Based on his current experience as a landlord and by reviewing recent advertisements online and in local newspapers for rental properties in the same general area, John believes that he can rent properties for between $1,400 and $1,600 per month depending on the actual square footage of each home and the number of bedrooms.
    c. Primary residence owners in Florida receive a homestead deduction for property taxes, so John increases the amount disclosed on the MLS listings to better reflect what he will need to pay for property taxes when renting each property.
    d. John has an estimate from his insurance agent for annual property insurance costs.
    e. John was provided with financing terms for 15- and 30-year fixed rate mortgages. He models both options to determine the most attractive financing.
    f. Some properties have periodic homeowners' association charges that are disclosed in their MLS listings. When applicable, John includes such costs in his profitability forecasts.
    g. John assumes an average repair cost of $200 per month. While he expects this number to be substantially less in most months, large repair bills for substantially greater dollar amounts can be unexpected and will ultimately be needed over time. Since John cannot pinpoint the timing or amounts of such items, for modeling purposes, he assumes an average monthly expense.
    h. Buying homes that have been occupied and preparing them for new tenants usually requires new paint and some general repairs. In addition, sometimes a house will need new carpeting as well. When doing the initial modeling, John assumes up-front costs of $3,000 to prepare each property for use. He assumes that any needed repair costs above this amount will be handled by the sellers or reflected in a lower purchase price.

8. Based on John's profitability forecasts for the four homes, he has an idea of which ones might provide the greatest profitability. However, he still needs to view each home interior and get a sense of its condition.
9. John's Realtor makes appointments to view the four homes. Based on the floor plans and the amount of work required, John drops another home from his list. He is now down to three.
10. In considering proper offering prices for each house, John discusses some recommendations with his Realtor. She provides some insights on each of the home sellers. One seller is moving to take a new job in another city and is very motivated to sell. Another couple is getting a divorce and also appears eager. There is little known about the circumstances surrounding the third sale. John tells his Realtor that he needs a day to come up with a proper initial offer.

Negotiation Process

John likes to maintain a sense of urgency when bidding for properties. He expends significant effort in selecting each home and he does not want to lose a property to other buyers. In addition, the more time a seller has, the higher the probability that other offers will be received and the greater a seller's negotiating position.

All three properties that John has considered are located within a few blocks of one another. Recent selling prices in these neighborhoods have averaged around $125 per square foot when considering the portion of the home that is under air conditioning and heating (i.e., garages and other unheated spaces do not count). John knows that because these are fairly generic residential properties, the most common method in determining value is the comparable sales approach. The three houses range from 1,500 to 1,650 square feet.

John can only afford to buy one of the three houses, which gives him some comfort in bidding somewhat low for each property. However, he realizes that current market conditions are probably more favorable toward sellers than buyers. John does not want to bid overly low and then be forced to provide a much higher bid in order to buy a property. Doing so could cause him to lose credibility and hurt his negotiating position. But the ownership of an unwanted property by a desperate seller can also be a motivating factor when considering an offer. John thinks about the sellers that are moving and divorcing.

John's first choice is the property owned by the divorcing couple. Its listing price is $126 per square foot, or $195,300 ($126 per square foot for a 1,550-square-foot home), which is the cheapest of the three properties. In addition, John likes the property best due to its cul-de-sac location, a secluded and large backyard, and the overall condition of the property.

John decides to offer a price of $110 per square foot for his favored property. This results in an initial bid of $170,500. John chooses to bid on one property at a time so that he does not mislead anyone or end up with more than one offer being accepted. However, to keep the process moving, John plans to require the seller to accept or reject his offer by 5:00 PM the following day.

John calls his Realtor to discuss the terms of the offer. She agrees with his approach. Other deal terms are clarified so that the Realtor can prepare the initial sales contract containing the offer. John is willing to provide an initial "good faith" deposit of $3,000 if the contract is accepted and close the transaction within 45 days. A maximum repair allowance is requested for up to $5,000 pending a home inspection. John knows that he can close within a few weeks and he does not expect repair costs to be above $2,000. John also has the right to revoke the contract and have any deposit returned based upon the results of a home inspection.

The initial contract gives John the right to have the property inspection performed within two weeks of final contract signing. John can have an inspection performed within a few days if needed. After doing so, a report will be provided to John that details any current and foreseeable problems with the property. Once in receipt of the report, John can accept the terms of the contract or try to renegotiate based on the results of the home inspection. If John accepts the terms after this two-week contingency period and does not purchase the home as promised for any reason, he will lose his deposit.

The seller's Realtor is responsive to the offer. Based on his sales commission, he is motivated to see the transaction close. The following morning John's Realtor receives a counteroffer at $120 per square foot or $186,000. Other items countered include a maximum repair allowance of $2,000, a shorter home inspection and contingency period and some other minor items, most of which John expected.

John and his Realtor view the seller's willingness to negotiate as a positive indication. John knows that he can buy the home at their countered offering price and meet his minimum projected profitability threshold. But he decides to have his Realtor provide a counteroffer and attempt to negotiate a lower price.

When discussing the counteroffer, John provides his Realtor with a list of items that he believes will be required to tenant the property. He mentions that he has a minimum profitability target that is based solely on numbers and that he cannot pay more than a certain price. Therefore, the counteroffer and the message conveyed should state a final offering price of $178,000 (which is about $115 per square foot). The sellers can accept this offer or John will need to move on to the next property.

John also has his Realtor mention that the roof on the property is almost 10 years old and that the heating and air conditioning system is dated as well. Lastly, after speaking to his lender and as an enticement to the sellers, John also commits to closing the transaction for the price of $178,000 within three weeks. The sellers are given until the next day to respond or John's counteroffer becomes invalid.

The next day the offer is accepted. John is pleased with the final terms of the transaction. After a final contract is signed, John arranges a home inspection. The results show a dozen relatively minor needed repairs, but nothing that would require renegotiation. The sellers are offered the option to make the repairs or to take another $1,650 off the closing price. They choose the latter and the deal is on track to close later in the month.

Property Management

While John is waiting to close the purchase of his fourth property, he begins reviewing his marketing process. He realizes that the sooner he leases the property, the less start-up cash he will need from his own pocket. John's first mortgage payment will not be due for at least 30 days post closing and his leases require the payment of each month's rent in advance. Therefore, if John can rent the property within 30 days of closing, the first month's rent will cover his first mortgage payment. Based on current demand in the market, John believes that this is an achievable goal.

John's lease requires the tenant to produce the first and last month's rent and a security deposit equal to one month's rent at the time of lease signing. The last month's rent and the security deposit will be held in a separate account with a local bank until needed. Some, all, or none of the security deposit may be returned to the tenant when the property is vacated depending upon its condition. In addition, the lease requires the tenant to properly maintain the landscaping and lawn and pay telephone and utility bills. Also, each of John's leases requires tenants to pay the first $50 of any repair bills. This makes it less likely that tenants will call for unnecessary repairs and more likely that they will fix things themselves and deal with repairmen directly for small items.

John prepares an advertisement for the local newspaper offering his new property for $1,550 per month. This means a tenant will need to provide a certified check for $4,650 before signing the lease (first and last month's rent and one month's security deposit). John is willing to enter a one-year lease at this price in order to attract a good tenant. At lease maturity, he hopes to raise the rental rate. Each prospective tenant will need to complete a brief application and pay a $30 fee associated with having a credit history report prepared to ensure adequate financial strength. John uses an Internet-based tenant screening company to perform this service.

John does not intend to make all of the repairs recommended in the home inspection report and expects fairly small repair costs to prepare the property for occupancy. He lines up his handyman to begin work the day after the scheduled closing. The handyman's work should be completed within a few days. At the same time, John schedules a painter to quickly spackle and paint the interior of the home. These total costs are expected to be around $1,800.

Other Considerations

Based on the final figures agreed to in the contract, John remodeled the projected profitability of his purchase. He was presented with financing options for 15- and 30-year mortgages. The interest rate was .30% lower for a 15-year mortgage, but this resulted in a substantially larger monthly payment, less cash flow to weather any unexpected events, and slightly lower projected profitability. Therefore, John decided to enter a 30-year fixed rate mortgage.

John was given the option of an adjustable rate loan. The interest rate was lower than both fixed rate alternatives. However, based upon John's current buy-and-hold investment strategy, he preferred to use fixed rate financing.

As indicated in Table 14.1, the estimated average annual return for John's fourth property assuming a five-year holding period and the assumptions included is approximately 14.76%. This means that under his current assumptions, John should earn an average return of approximately 14.76% each year that he holds the property. John hopes that his assumptions are conservative and that his actual profits will be substantially higher based upon greater appreciation, higher rents, and lower costs.

John realizes that he may sell the property within five years or hold it indefinitely. In addition, he knows that some of his assumptions may vary significantly over the years to come. But by evaluating the potential profitability of the property prior to purchase and making sure that the numbers make sense, John is maintaining a rational and disciplined investment strategy that is lacked by many real estate investors.

Table 14.1
Real Estate Acquisitions Model: Average Annual Profitability Forecast

	AVERAGE ANNUAL EXPECTED RETURN	14.76%
Compute		

ASSUMPTIONS

APPRECIATION & SALE OF PROPERTY

2	Average Annual Appreciation Rate	4.00%
3	Repair Costs to Prepare Property for Sale at End of Year 5 (% of Sales Price)	0.50%
4	Realtor Commissions at Time of Sale (% of Sales Price)	5.00%
5	Non-Realtor Closing Costs at Time of Sale (taxes, title agency, etc.) (% of Sales Price)	0.50%

FINANCING & CLOSING COSTS

6	Purchase Price ($)	$ 176,350	Loan Amount	$ 141,080
7	Mortgage Loan-to-Value (%)	80.00%	Equity/Down payment	$ 35,270
8	Annual Interest Rate (%)	6.00%		
9	Monthly Mortgage Term (used for amortization)	360		
10	Loan and Property Closing Costs ($)	$ 1,250		
11	Upfront Costs Required to Prepare for Occupancy ($)	$ 1,800		

EXPENSES

		Year 1	Year 2	Year 3	Year 4	Year 5
12	Average Monthly Insurance	$ 75	$ 75	$ 80	$ 80	$ 85
13	Average Monthly Real Estate Taxes	$ 250	$ 275	$ 275	$ 300	$ 300
14	Average Monthly Homeowners' Association Dues	$ 15	$ 16	$ 17	$ 17	$ 18
15	Average Monthly Repair Costs	$ 200	$ 200	$ 200	$ 200	$ 200
16	Other Monthly Expense 1	$ -	$ -	$ -	$ -	$ -
17	Other Monthly Expense 2	$ -	$ -	$ -	$ -	$ -
18	Other Monthly Expense 3	$ -	$ -	$ -	$ -	$ -
19	Other Monthly Expense 4	$ -	$ -	$ -	$ -	$ -
20	Other Monthly Expense 5	$ -	$ -	$ -	$ -	$ -

1 RENTAL INCOME

Month 1	$ 1,550	Month 31	$ 1,600
Month 2	$ 1,550	Month 32	$ 1,600
Month 3	$ 1,550	Month 33	$ 1,600
Month 4	$ 1,550	Month 34	$ 1,600
Month 5	$ 1,550	Month 35	$ 1,600
Month 6	$ 1,550	Month 36	$ 1,600
Month 7	$ 1,550	Month 37	$ 1,600
Month 8	$ 1,550	Month 38	$ 1,625
Month 9	$ 1,550	Month 39	$ 1,625
Month 10	$ 1,550	Month 40	$ 1,625
Month 11	$ 1,550	Month 41	$ 1,625
Month 12	$ 1,550	Month 42	$ 1,625
Month 13	$ 1,575	Month 43	$ 1,625
Month 14	$ 1,575	Month 44	$ 1,625
Month 15	$ 1,575	Month 45	$ 1,625
Month 16	$ 1,575	Month 46	$ 1,625
Month 17	$ 1,575	Month 47	$ 1,625
Month 18	$ 1,575	Month 48	$ 1,625
Month 19	$ 1,575	Month 49	$ 1,625
Month 20	$ 1,575	Month 50	$ 1,625
Month 21	$ 1,575	Month 51	$ 1,625
Month 22	$ 1,575	Month 52	$ 1,625
Month 23	$ 1,575	Month 53	$ 1,625
Month 24	$ 1,575	Month 54	$ 1,625
Month 25	$ -	Month 55	$ 1,625
Month 26	$ 1,600	Month 56	$ 1,625
Month 27	$ 1,600	Month 57	$ 1,625
Month 28	$ 1,600	Month 58	$ 1,625
Month 29	$ 1,600	Month 59	$ -
Month 30	$ 1,600	Month 60	$ -

As John considers his total portfolio of four properties, he strives to layer the length and maturity dates of each lease to significantly reduce the risk of having one or more properties vacant at the same time. His immediate goal is to have all four lease maturity dates end at least three months apart. Assuming all tenants honor their full lease terms, this will give John ample opportunity to re-tenant each property without adversely disrupting his total portfolio cash flow each month.

Conclusion

John's long-term strategy of buying and holding properties in attractive neighborhoods having strong demographic trends has proven successful to date. The fact that he was able to refinance an existing property and buy another has helped to increase his profit potential and expand his portfolio. John may decide to sell one or more properties at some point in the future if he believes that his target market is becoming overheated. But for the foreseeable future, John intends to slowly and methodically continue buying properties and adding to his portfolio.

John's experience with prior property ownership and management has helped tremendously with the purchase of his fourth property. He now has an established network of relationships that can assist him when assessing market conditions and specific properties, while also providing an array of reliable and fairly priced services.

John understands direct residential real estate investing and is maintaining a sound and prudent investment strategy.

CASE STUDY II

Investor:	Cindy Morgan
Occupation:	Auto mechanic
Real estate experience:	Owns one property in Norwalk, Connecticut
Property management:	Third-party property management firm
Primary investment strategy:	Buy-and-hold/time the market
Current market conditions:	Overheated and peaked from rapid appreciation; beginnings of a down market

Overview

Cindy inherited a single-family home from her mother about four years ago. Rather than sell it, she decided to find a tenant and hold the property as an investment. Cindy is grateful for this decision since housing prices have risen dramatically since she took ownership of the property. She has been contemplating the purchase of an additional property for the past two years, but based upon her profitability assumptions, high home prices have made it difficult to find suitable investment opportunities.

Market Assessment

Housing prices in Norwalk have experienced rapid appreciation over the past five years. Some media sources have been predicting a housing bust for the past two years. While Cindy's initial investment strategy was based upon a buy-and-hold approach, she is concerned that signs of a declining market will result in more severe down market conditions than many people are expecting. Based on the current state of the market, Cindy has decided not to purchase any additional residential real estate and to sell her rental property. She has based her decisions on the following factors:

- The average annual appreciation rate for housing in Norwalk has averaged over 10% per year for the past five years.
- Numerous real estate speculators have been active within the residential real estate market purchasing and selling single-family homes; it is apparent that people without rational investment strategies are attempting to time the market by buying and quickly selling houses.
- The average number of monthly home sales in Norwalk has been steadily decreasing over the past six months.
- The inventory of homes on the market has been gradually increasing. During the past five years, the level of home inventories on the market had narrowed to as low as two months. However, based on recent homes sales for the past six or seven months, the Norwalk market is approaching six months worth of inventory. Cindy realizes that home inventories can swing back and forth due to seasonal factors, but she believes that this trend will continue and worsen.
- During recent years, it has taken on average only a couple months to sell a home. However, during the past year, the average time a house remains on the market has increased to over five months and the trend has steadily been increasing.
- Housing prices in the general area seem to have peaked and started to decline as motivated sellers are dropping prices to compete with one another.
- The affordability of housing has been decreasing each year for the past six years. In addition, the percentage of people renting homes in the city has been increasing.
- Interest rates have been historically low for a number of years. Banks and other lenders have been aggressively competing and offering creative financing terms.

Valuation

Cindy has looked at dozens of properties on and off during the past two years. Each time she forecasts the profitability of a potential property, the average annual expected return is in the single digits. These numbers have continued to drop even more as prices have risen further and rental rates have lagged behind. Cindy's last profitability forecast showed only a 2% average annual expected return assuming 5% average annual appreciation.

Based on ongoing failed attempts to find suitably priced investment properties, Cindy has concluded that the Norwalk residential real estate market is over-heated. Under a best-case scenario, Cindy expects the market to flatten. But based upon recent trends, she believes that some type of pricing correction will be needed to make housing more affordable.

Cindy decides not to buy another property and to sell her existing property. She believes it best to exit the residential real estate market, continue watching market trends, and consider reentering the market when the numbers make more sense.

Cindy realizes that home prices may continue increasing and that she may lose potential profits by selling if the market keeps rising. She also realizes that a substantial marketing period is generally required to sell illiquid assets such as real estate and that by the time her property sells, prices may have declined further.

But Cindy knows that she cannot time the market perfectly and that her investment has performed extremely well, especially since she leveraged the property shortly after the inheritance. After receiving the home, Cindy obtained a loan from a local bank. Because there was no prior debt on the property, Cindy was able to take all of the cash proceeds from the loan and purchase a diversified portfolio of mutual funds.

Property Management

When Cindy first decided to rent the house that she inherited, she chose to hire a property management firm to manage the property. The cost of this service is 10% of monthly rent and includes any time expended by the firm to re-tenant the property. Cindy received a lower fee estimate from another property management firm, but the proven experience and stellar reputation of the firm she chose seemed worth the additional cost.

When selecting a property management firm, Cindy targeted a local company managing additional properties within the same neighborhoods as her rental unit. She wanted a firm that was familiar with her specific market and that specialized in residential property management.

By using an experienced property management firm, Cindy benefited from having all of the responsibilities associated with direct real estate ownership handled by a professional service provider. By doing so, Cindy felt assured that rents would be priced appropriately and that leases would be secure and compliant.

Cindy receives a statement each month outlining the various revenues and expenses associated with her property. The property management firm pays the expenses associated with the property, including Cindy's monthly mortgage payments, and deposits any remaining proceeds directly into Cindy's bank account each month.

Cindy's second tenant required eviction after consistently failing to pay his rent on time. The property management firm handled this process by working with a local real estate attorney. The firm was able to keep costs reasonably low while taking care of the eviction, the oversight of some needed repairs, and the finding of a new tenant.

Cindy realizes that by self-managing her property she could potentially increase the profitability of her investment. However, she feels equally compensated by the peace of mind and additional free time received from the use of a property management firm.

Selling Commissions

Cindy's property management firm also assists her with the sale of her property and agrees to do so using a discounted commission schedule based upon her existing relationship. Cindy asked for references from the sellers of the last three homes sold by the firm. All spoke highly of the firm's capabilities and level of service.

Because the market is still considered to be very active, the property management firm agreed to a 5% selling commission. Of this amount, 3% will be awarded to the buyer's real estate agent and the remaining 2% will be kept by the property management firm upon the sale of the property. If the property management firm finds the buyer, which is very possible considering that its clients are always seeking new investment properties, they will earn an extra 2% (4% commissions in total) rather than the 3% that would normally be paid to a third-party buyer's agent. If this happens, Cindy will only be paying a 4% commission rather than 5%.

Marketing/Negotiation

Since listing the property, there has been fairly strong demand based on the number of viewings. In addition, Cindy received two offers within the first few weeks, but she and her Realtor both agreed to seek a higher price. Both offers seemed to be from speculators trying to purchase properties at a discount for investment purposes.

Throughout the sales process, Cindy has been impressed by many of the strategies employed by her Realtor, including the following:

- After Cindy's tenant moved out, general repairs were made, the carpets were cleaned, and some of the walls were repainted to make the property more marketable and in anticipation of the ultimate buyer's home inspection. A portion of these costs were covered by some of the prior tenant's security deposit.
- A detailed and well-written color marketing brochure was created that stresses the positive aspects of the home, including new and unique features that should attract the attention of potential buyers.
- The Realtor strives to create as much demand as possible by listing the home on MLS and the company's Web site and by placing the sales sign and marketing brochures prominently in front of the house. In addition, an open house event was hosted by the Realtor on a Saturday afternoon and listing information was faxed or mailed to all the Realtors in the area.
- When considering offers on the home, the Realtor focuses Cindy's attention on key information about each potential buyer. For example, comments from other Realtors such as "the wife really loves the house" or "the father's friends live on the same block" are favorable indications when considering a counteroffer.
- When talking to other Realtors, Cindy's Realtor stresses the fact that Cindy maintains low leverage on the home and has the ability to hold the property long term. She also casually mentions that Cindy is debating between selling and re-tenanting the home.
- Cindy's Realtor tends to exaggerate the level of competing interest in the property when talking to other Realtors.
- When contracts are being negotiated, Cindy's Realtor focuses on large deposits and on minimizing contingency periods in order to lock in as much of a buyer's money as soon as possible. She knows that buyers are much less likely to walk away from a deal once their deposits are at risk.

Cindy and her Realtor remain optimistic that the property will be sold fairly quickly at a solid price. There is still significant activity from home buyers and from investors that expect the market to continue rising. While Cindy wishes to sell before market conditions worsen, she does not want to leave a substantial amount of money on the table by selling too quickly. She and her Realtor are seeking a balance between these two objectives.

Summary

Cindy's initial strategy was to buy and hold one or more properties. However, as the local residential real estate market began to overheat, she decided to try and time the market by selling her existing investment and by avoiding the purchase of an additional property. By using reasonable assumptions and determining that residential real estate prices no longer made sense, Cindy maintained a degree of logic and discipline. In rising markets, greed can dominate the mentality of many investors trying to perfectly time markets and squeeze every dollar of profit from their investments.

Cindy understands the benefits of real estate ownership and that prices continue to trend upward over the long term. But she also recognizes that when an overheated market corrects, a substantial amount of her equity can be lost for many years.

Cindy may not time her sale perfectly. The current market has clearly started to soften and she still needs to find a buyer. But Cindy believes that current pricing and liquidity are still much better when compared to upcoming market conditions. Based upon her passive strategy and current market assessment, Cindy may avoid real estate investing for the near to mid-term or longer depending on the extent and timing of any market correction. But she believes that now is the time to sell and that increasing pricing pressure and greater housing inventory and illiquidity will present great buying opportunities in the future.

CASE STUDY III

Investor:	Jim Daily
Occupation:	Mechanical engineer
Real estate experience:	Successfully bought, improved, and sold several properties during the past few years in Modesto, California
Property management:	Self-managed
Primary investment strategy:	Property improvement
Current market conditions:	Flat market with little activity

Overview

Jim's investment strategy is based upon buying, improving, and then selling properties. He generally looks for unattractive houses that do not show well to potential buyers. Jim is not looking to perform major or lengthy renovations. Rather, his targeted properties are structurally sound, but generally need significant cosmetic work to enhance their appeal.

Property Selection

Jim recently visited a vacant home that he is considering for investment. The house has been on the market for about a year. It resides in an attractive neighborhood, but needs a substantial amount of work. Many people have looked at the property, but no one has had the willingness or initiative to take on the project.

The house has no landscaping. Any remnants of a lawn consist of scattered portions of dead grass and weeds throughout the yard and surrounding the house. The paint on the home is badly chipped and pealing and sections of dry wood are abundantly visible. The interior of the home is dismal and dirty with a foul and moldy smell. The carpeting, window dressings, and appliances are ruined, toilets and sinks are stained, and there is a need for numerous smaller repairs throughout the house.

While most buyers would not even bother to look inside the home, the asking price was low enough to attract Jim's attention. In addition, the home was built extremely well with high-quality materials. When visiting the property, Jim took detailed notes of everything he thought the home needed to become marketable. A copy of Jim's initial list is included in Table 14.2.

Based on Jim's initial estimate, he concluded that $42,500 would be enough money to convert an ugly duckling into a swan. The asking price for the home is $150,000. More desirable homes in the area of comparable size are selling for around $280,000. But Jim realizes that his financing options for such an acquisition are probably limited, which means that he will probably have to invest more of his own money than if he were buying a better conditioned property. In

Table 14.2
Estimated Renovation Costs—312 Mayberry Street

Item	Estimated Cost
Sod installation	$ 8,000
Landscaping	2,000
Tree pruning and removal	1,500
Sprinkler system repair	600
Power wash driveway	150
Exterior wood replacement	1,250
New roof	8,500
Paint exterior	4,000
Spackle and paint interior	1,500
New carpeting	2,000
New appliances	1,500
Window dressings	1,200
New kitchen countertop	750
Bathroom retiling	2,000
Two new toilets, sinks, and countertops	800
Three sets of new closet doors	750
Heating and air conditioning service	500
General electrical repairs	1,000
General handyman repairs	4,000
Cleaning service	500
Total	$ 42,500

addition, the residential real estate markets are stagnant and selling the property could take a while and a substantial discount might be required.

Because this dilapidated property has been on the market so long, Jim believes that he can negotiate a purchase price significantly below the current asking price. Jim also realizes that the quality and level of detail of a home inspection will be critical when deciding whether to make the acquisition. If a contract is signed, adequate contingency times would be needed for the home inspection and for obtaining financing.

Financing

As Jim's interest in the project increases, he decides to speak to a few lenders about potential financing. In order to make the project feasible, Jim needs a lender to lend not only against the current property value but also on the additional value that will ultimately be provided by the planned renovations.

Jim has initial conversations with three lenders. Jim describes the project and reviews his expense assumptions with representatives from each firm. He also talks about current selling prices in the neighborhood for similar homes. Jim acknowledges that the local residential real estate market has been fairly inactive and flat. But he also mentions that his profitability assumptions assume an extended marketing period. In addition, the expected profit in the venture should allow a substantial discount to the selling price if needed. Lastly, the fact that so many features of the house will be brand new upon completion of the renovations should make the home stand out from its peers.

Jim has proven his ability to buy, improve, and sell other properties. In addition, he presents himself in a professional manner and thoroughly researches each project. But one lender shows little interest and another seems to have significant hurdles to overcome before being able to provide an indication of interest. A loan officer within Jim's local bank knows Jim and expresses a willingness to try and move forward. After briefly talking to her manager, she provides Jim with some rough financing terms that she thinks would be achievable pending an appraisal and other detailed information about the property, the planned expenditures, and the ultimate sale assumptions.

Because the property is in such a deteriorated condition and has little marketability in its current state, the bank is reluctant to lend money against the planned renovations without some restrictions. Based on Jim's fairly short-term investment strategy, the bank suggests providing Jim an interest-only, two-year loan with a fixed interest rate of 7.5%. Based on the assumed purchase price of $135,000 used in the information that John provided to the bank, the maximum loan amount would be $155,000. However, Jim could only initially borrow $110,000 to buy the property and the remaining $45,000 would be borrowed in stages as the renovations were completed. An employee from the bank would periodically visit the property to ensure that progress was being made and that the ultimate value of the bank's underlying collateral was steadily increasing.

Jim thanks his banker for her time and for the valuable feedback. He can now take the financing assumptions and further refine his profitability estimates. But Jim also needs to consider the source of his remaining financing. He does not have tens of thousands of dollars in available cash. However, Jim does have access to additional debt.

Jim maintains a line of credit secured by the equity in his primary residence that allows him to borrow up to $70,000. He can borrow and repay the loan at anytime in small increments. Jim has almost 15 years remaining on the loan, so as long as he does not sell his primary residence, he does not need to worry about the loan maturing or becoming due in the near future. However, Jim does need to make monthly interest payments on any amounts borrowed. This home equity line could serve as Jim's second source of capital to cover the shortfall between the total amount of cash needed and the loan amount that the bank is willing to provide.

Assuming that Jim uses debt provided by the bank and his home equity loan to finance his project, he will be employing 100% leverage. The higher the leverage on a project, the greater the risks. But such a high degree of leverage would also increase the profit potential on the project significantly.

Jim also knows that there will be no cash flow being generated from the property. He could always maintain holding power by renting the property once it is finished and refinance with a more traditional and longer term loan, but this would tie up his capital for much longer than he would like and halt his current investment strategy. Jim only has enough money to purchase one property at a time. If he purchases this property, he will need to sell it before moving on to the next.

Jim likes to be very conservative when estimating the profitability of each project. He believes that he can reduce his initial repair cost estimates, but he decides to use the higher numbers when forecasting profitability. Jim also needs to consider how long he will own the property and the associated holding costs for this period. Jim wants to be absolutely sure that he has adequate financing to cover the project and make all the necessary payments.

Based on the information gathered to date, Jim estimates his cash outflows and financing needs in Table 14.3. While he expects to complete the needed renovations and sell the property within 9 to 10 months, Jim assumes an 18-month holding period when estimating the costs associated with making his loan, insurance, utility, and property tax payments. In addition, he assumes another $5,000 for contingency expenses to cover any unexpected problems that may arise. Jim wants to make sure that the project is still attractive under conservative assumptions.

As indicated in Table 14.3, under the current assumptions, Jim would need to borrow $57,112 on his home equity line of credit during the life of the project in order to renovate and carry it for 18 months. Now that he believes he can raise an appropriate amount of capital to complete the project, Jim's next step is to assess whether or not the potential profit is worthwhile.

Valuation

Based on recent home sales in the same and adjacent neighborhoods, similar sized houses have been selling for about $280,000. When estimating total project profitability, Jim assumes the sales price and selling costs listed in Table 14.4.

Based on a sales price of $265,000, normal Realtor and closing expenses, and the total project costs assumed in Table 14.4, Jim believes that he can earn a profit of at

Table 14.3
Estimated Cash Outflows and Financing Needs—312 Mayberry Street

Project expenses		
Purchase price	$	135,000
Plus: Renovation costs		42,500
Bank financing payments		17,000
Home equity loan payments		5,000
Power and water costs		2,700
Insurance costs		2,000
Property taxes		2,912
Contingencies		5,000
Total costs	$	212,112
Project financing		
Bank financing	$	155,000
Home equity loan		57,112
Total financing	$	212,112

least $35,663 after buying, improving, and selling the home. This would be quite a windfall considering that he would not be using any of his own money.

Jim gains comfort from his assumptions. He believes that his actual expenses can be substantially less based upon a shorter holding period and lower renovation costs. In addition, even though the local residential real estate market is currently experiencing little activity, he thinks that the selling price of the home is attractive based upon all of the planned replacements.

Negotiation

Feeling comfortable with the project, Jim contacts his Realtor to create the terms of an offer. Since the home has been for sale for over a year and the price

Table 14.4
Estimated Profitability—312 Mayberry Street

Sales price	$	265,000
Less: Realtor commissions (6%)		(15,900)
Closing costs (0.5%)		(1,325)
Net sales price		247,775
Less: Total costs		(212,112)
Total profit	$	35,663

has been reduced twice in an effort to sell, Jim wants to make a lowball offer.

Jim's Realtor has had preliminary discussions with the seller's Realtor about the potential for an offer. The seller's Realtor stated that the seller has no debt on the property, which has given her the ability to hold the property for over a year. However, she is eager to sell. The seller's Realtor also tells Jim's Realtor that the seller has not received any offers for the past nine months. Jim is surprised that the seller's Realtor would release this information, but it makes him consider an even lower initial bid.

Jim provides a list of the items that need to be repaired and replaced to his Realtor and asks that he review the items with the seller's Realtor to ensure that the seller is aware of how bad the home's condition really is. He includes some items on the list that are aged even though he does not plan to replace them, such as the heating and air conditioning system. In addition, Jim's Realtor also mentions the risks involved with such a project during a flat and stagnant stage of the real estate market in which normal homes are taking approximately eight months to sell. Jim also stresses to his Realtor to convey the fact that he is an investor and that the numbers dictate his decisions.

After a series of bids and conversations between Realtors debating over the pricing and the amount of work required to renovate the home, a purchase price of $125,000 is agreed upon. Jim is pleased. This is $10,000 lower than the purchase price he assumed for his modeling, which will lead to even greater profits or allow Jim to sell the house at an even lower price if needed.

The contract also provides for a closing date within 60 days and contingencies for financing and home inspections. Jim has 30 days to obtain a financing commitment and receive one or more home inspections. Because of the complexity of the project, he wants enough time to order and review detailed home inspections and receive actual bids for the major repair and renovation items. Jim also wants the home tested for mold and insect damage.

As Jim solidifies his numbers, he will continue to work with his relationship manager at the bank toward a formal financing commitment. Jim refines his cost estimates and submits them to the bank with written estimates from third-party service providers. He also provides the bank with his profitability calculations and stresses the conservatism within his assumptions.

Because of the long contingency period and extended closing date, the seller requested a deposit of $5,000, which Jim accepted. If Jim is unable to receive a financing commitment within 30 days or if one or more home inspections reveal unexpected problems with the property within the same period, Jim can cancel the contract and have his deposit returned. After the 30-day contingency period, Jim is obligated to buy the home or lose his deposit.

Other Considerations

Once Jim closes the transaction and purchases the home, his team of repair and service professionals will begin work immediately. Jim chose not to perform any of the repairs himself. Rather, he will oversee the progress and timely completion of each task. Jim will need to manage costs in detail to ensure that they adhere to their original estimates. If unexpected expenses arise, Jim needs to understand the underlying reasons. Jim also needs to proactively try to reduce costs whenever possible.

Once the renovations are complete, Jim will have his Realtor list the property for sale. Jim will want to sell the property fast to eliminate the negative monthly cash flow being generated by the property and to repay his loans. However, he does not want to sell the property too quickly and be forced to significantly discount the sales price. Jim will need to find a balance when setting the initial listing price and when considering offers and counteroffers.

After Jim sells the property, he plans to ultimately use the profits to invest in another residential property. Jim feels comfortable investing in single-family homes based on his past successes and a relatively simplistic investment strategy when compared to other forms of direct real estate investing. Because Jim is adding value to each property that he acquires, he believes that he can make money by using such a strategy in any real estate market. Jim realizes that it may take a substantial amount of time to find each property, but he plans to exercise patience and target what he perceives to be lower risk projects.

Summary

Jim expended significant time and effort before deciding to bid on the property and before signing a contract. His work continued for the weeks to follow during the contingency period to ensure that his figures were accurate and that there were no unexpected problems associated with the home. This level of diligence has provided Jim with a substantial profit opportunity.

Chapter 15

COMMERCIAL REAL ESTATE INVESTING

THE NEED FOR GREATER EXPERTISE

Commercial properties include retail strip centers and stand-alone buildings, offices, hotels, retirement facilities, warehouses, industrial buildings, and other types of real estate usually being used for some type of business activity. Multifamily structures that contain more than four units are also considered commercial properties, since the complexities of owning such types of investments increase substantially when compared to smaller residential properties.

Most investors in commercial real estate are REITs and other well-capitalized real estate investment companies, particularly when it comes to the larger and more expensive properties. This is because many commercial properties can cost tens of millions of dollars and require large amounts of cash to cover maintenance and repair costs and vacancy time. In addition, real estate companies employ professionals that specialize in the skills needed to manage and oversee specific types of commercial properties. Also, by owning many of the same types of properties, efficiencies can result by spreading corporate overhead costs and expertise across a large number of assets.

There are clearly more risks associated with commercial real estate investing when compared to residential real estate investing. Commercial real estate vacancy times can be significantly longer and commercial market downturns can be more common and prolonged when compared to residential markets. In addition, commercial tenants often require owners to pay for renovations to meet their specific needs or they may require substantial rent concessions to cover some or all of these costs before moving into a property.

One of the greatest risks associated with commercial properties is due to their specificity of use. Chances are that you will not be able to lease office space to a restaurant owner or replace a tenant in your warehouse other than with another warehouse operator. Many commercial real estate markets move in cycles. For example, the demand for office space can vary significantly based upon local, regional, and national variables such as the state of the economy or specific industries. Factory and industrial tenants may leave a certain area in search of cheaper labor or better proximity to suppliers. You also have the credit risk of individual operators. If the clothing store renting your property goes out of business, you just lost a tenant.

Commercial real estate is an illiquid asset that can require substantial amounts of cash to maintain. Due to the limitations of use for many types of properties, vacancies can last for years. Many of us have seen vacant storefronts or gas stations in our neighborhoods remain vacant for long periods of time. Owners are paying taxes, insurance, debt payments, and other costs to maintain these properties while earning no offsetting income.

The leases on commercial properties are more complex than those used for residential properties. These are more formal legal agreements that often require the services of an attorney for advice and review. Each lease with each tenant is a separately negotiated instrument and usually serves as collateral for any lender financing provided to the property owner.

There is clearly a greater level of property management, leasing, and financing experience required to purchase, tenant, and manage commercial properties. It takes years to accumulate this level of expertise. In addition, specific markets should be researched for vacancy trends, comparable pricing and rents, potential growth or contraction outlooks, etc.

But taking large bets on commercial properties at the right time can generate huge payoffs. Buying a commercial property when rents are low or vacancies are high can lead to great profits if an investor can increase NOI and enhance the property's value.

Assume that an investor purchases a 25-unit apartment building when the residential housing market is booming, financing is cheap and easy to obtain, and demand for apartments is relatively low since a large number of people are able to afford to buy homes. The demand for apartments and other types of rental properties often has an inverse relationship with the state of the housing market. When more people can buy homes, there are fewer renters. This leads to lower demand for apartments, which causes higher vacancy rates. Owners of apartment buildings will try to increase occupancy by lowering rents. Low rents and high vacancies result in reduced rental income and lower NOI.

Table 15.1 shows the NOI calculation for a hypothetical 25-unit apartment building. The table assumes that this apartment building is being valued using an 8% capitalization rate. To determine an estimate of value today, the property's NOI is divided by the 8% capitalization rate ($123,100 divided by 8%). This results in a value today for the property of approximately $1,538,750.

Now let us assume that the residential housing market peaks and is no longer affordable to many buyers. This causes people to start leaving the market. Also assume that lender financing becomes much more stringent as borrowers begin defaulting on the mortgages used to buy their high-priced homes. Now fewer people are going to purchase homes and more people are going to rent apartments and houses.

Under these assumptions, assume that an investor purchased the 25-unit apartment building at a price of $1,538,750 and over a two-year period was able to

Table 15.1
NOI Improvement Scenario—25-Unit Apartment Building

	Today	Two Years Later
Rental income	$ 180,000	$ 240,000
Maintenance costs	(9,000)	(15,000)
Repair costs	(30,000)	(35,000)
Property management	(14,400)	(19,200)
Professional fees	(3,500)	(5,000)
Net operating income	$ 123,100	$ 165,800
Net capitalization rate	8.00%	8.00%
Property value	$ 1,538,750	$ 2,072,500

increase occupancy levels and rental rates so that NOI was increased by about 35%. Using the same 8% capitalization rate, the property is now worth approximately $2,072,500.

Based on Table 15.1, the investor made a profit of $533,750 by buying, improving, and selling the property within a two-year period. If the investor used leverage to purchase the majority of the property, the profitability of this investment would have increased manyfold.

For example, if the investor put down 20% of his own money to purchase the property for $1,538,750, his initial investment would have been about $307,750 (20% times $1,538,750). His profit of $533,750 from the sale results in a 173.4% return on his investment ($533,750 divided by $307,750) over a two-year period. This simplification ignores any monthly cash flow received by the investor while owning the property. Assuming he was able to cover his debt payments and receive positive net cash flow in most months, his profits would be even higher.

Owning commercial real estate also provides investors with more opportunities to participate in real estate investing. As mentioned, there are numerous and varying types of commercial properties. By considering commercial real estate, an investor's investment opportunities can be expanded significantly.

There may be times when residential markets are overheated and buying opportunities are scarce. Depending upon your investment strategy, you may be a seller of residential properties during certain market cycles. If the numbers do not make sense, rather than purchase properties at inflated prices, you may sit on the sidelines for a significant period of time waiting for market pricing to correct and decline to more sustainable levels. During such periods when residential investments are limited, commercial real estate may be much more attractive.

My suggestion for the average investor is to maintain portfolio diversification and stick to single-family homes before perhaps eventually graduating to duplexes, triplexes, and small apartment buildings. For those of you that want to enter the commercial real estate market, consider starting with fairly inexpensive properties having simplistic lease structures and the ability to be marketed to a diverse group of tenants.

DIRECT COMMERCIAL REAL ESTATE OWNERSHIP

The complexities of commercial real estate investing can vary dramatically depending upon an investor's investment strategy, targeted property type, and investment size. Large-scale commercial real estate investing and development should be handled by experts that specialize in these fields. However, individuals can participate in commercial real estate ownership on a smaller scale.

We have discussed some of the most common ways to indirectly invest in commercial real estate through passive investment strategies such as through REIT, TIC, LP, and LLC ownership. Such investments allow experienced professionals to choose and manage your investments. For those investors that want to advance to direct commercial property ownership, a gradual progression should be considered.

After mastering and fully understanding all of the nuances of residential real estate, investors should take small steps when entering the world of commercial real estate. While the level of risk and intricacy will vary by property and circumstance, there are some general ways that investors can methodically transition between residential and commercial real estate investing.

START WITH SMALL PROPERTIES

Bigger properties usually come with more expense and complexity. Greater amounts of debt are used to purchase more expensive properties, which results in larger monthly mortgage payments. In addition, repair and maintenance costs on such properties can be substantial as well. When large properties are vacant and no cash flow is being produced, investors must have adequate means to cover these cash outflows. By owning one or more smaller properties, such risks can be reduced.

There are advantages and disadvantages associated with owning larger properties. Unless you have a very large portfolio or you purchase small and inexpensive properties, putting substantial amounts of your invested funds into one property can result in poor diversification. This can lead to greater risks when compared to portfolios consisting of several or numerous properties.

Many smaller properties can be found having only one tenant. Other small properties may have up to a few tenants, which can help to diversify rental streams (i.e., when one tenant vacates another two may continue to lease). The fewer the tenants, the simpler the property management function. Most commercial properties require the services of an experienced property manager. However, for many smaller properties, investors can often eliminate the need for a property manager by leasing to strong tenants and by shifting many of the responsibilities associated with property ownership to the tenant.

PROPERTY LOCATION

To state the obvious, the current and future value of a property is highly contingent upon its location. Investors should be cognizant of what is happening within their target investment area. Lax zoning and use regulations may not be representative of future limitations. In addition, those areas with loose zoning and use laws may ultimately result in poorly planned and undesirable communities.

When assessing a property, remember to consider site access, the amount and direction of traffic flow, and the demographic trends of the area. Consider what else might be built in a given area based upon current and expected growth trends. For example, many parcels of real estate across the country have increased in value exponentially after an upcoming Wal-Mart was announced in the general area because of the expected traffic base that normally accompanies this brand.

Consider the supply and demand relationship of a target market. Areas that have substantial undeveloped land leave room for additional development. In such cases, there is clearly the potential for supply to outweigh demand. This can lead to overbuilding and downward pressure on real estate values. In desirable areas having limited or no available land, supply is constrained. Such circumstances can help to sustain and increase demand for property in the area.

THE STRENGTH OF THE TENANT

Credit-worthy and responsible tenants are desired when leasing both residential and commercial properties. However, this becomes even more important when owning and leasing commercial property. Residential properties are more generic and there is a greater abundance of potential tenants. In addition, assuming that you do not have destructive tenants, preparing a residence for occupancy between tenants is relatively inexpensive.

But commercial properties are used to run businesses and businesses often have customized branding and particular characteristics that help them stand out and attract customers. Signage and other features are often required under franchise agreements as well. This often entails renovating commercial space to meet the needs of each specific tenant.

Because of the uniqueness of each tenant and their individualistic needs, re-tenanting a commercial property can be expensive. In addition, finding new tenants, particularly during depressed market cycles, can take time and result in negative cash flow for extended periods. Therefore, investors want to avoid losing tenants and being forced to re-tenant properties.

The credit strength of each tenant is a critical consideration when leasing commercial property. For example, Jack-in-the-Box, Inc. might be operating one of its restaurants and guaranteeing the lease on your property. In this case, you have the credit strength of a publicly traded company that manages or owns over 2,000 restaurants guaranteeing the payments on your lease. However, one of the company's franchisees that owns and operates only a few restaurants under the same brand would be a much riskier tenant.

When looking to buy or when deciding to sell a commercial property, consider the track record of the tenant. Investors can lower their risk with properties leased to tenants having lucrative and stable businesses. If you buy a property with a brand new building leased to a new store operator, the level of your tenant's success is unproven and uncertain. The stability of such a tenant would provide significantly less assurance than a store operator that has been successfully operating in the same location for the past 10 years.

Also consider the industry of your tenants. People will continue to buy inexpensively priced food during varying economic conditions. However, people may not visit high-end restaurants during economic downturns. Nor will they buy as many luxury items.

When acquiring commercial properties with existing leases, buyers should request several years of financial statements reflecting the performance of the business. I usually ask for five years of profit-and-loss statements and I am usually willing to accept three. I also want to see at least the last two years of tax returns to ensure that there is not a material difference between what is being reported in the financial statements and what is being provided to the IRS.

Many commercial leases require tenants to submit quarterly or annual financial statements to their landlords so that the condition of their businesses can be assessed from period to period. Property owners like to be proactive and know when their tenant's business operations are beginning to show weakness. Trends for sales, labor, and other expenses can be very telling. If you do not feel comfortable reviewing financial statements, a local accountant or property management firm can help you to interpret the results.

GENERALITY OF USE

Because many commercial properties are customized to meet the needs of specific types of businesses, the universe of potential tenants for such properties can be limited. In addition, the particular location of a property will often confine its potential uses. Some businesses choose specific sites based upon the needs and locations of their targeted customers. Others select certain areas to maximize distribution efficiencies and to minimize costs. Each business has its own individualistic objectives when choosing a location.

The pool of potential tenants is much narrower when dealing with commercial properties compared to residential properties. This can be a concerning aspect of commercial real estate investing. The goals of receiving a strong and reliable rental stream and minimizing tenant turnover are more likely achieved when there is robust demand for a particular property and location. The more people that want something, the greater the demand they create. When there are few buyers and renters for a specific piece of property due to its limited uses, then there is less demand. Lower demand often translates into lower rents, property values, and appreciation potential.

Investors should consider the breadth of potential uses that each commercial property can provide. This is especially true when properties have existing or proposed tenants with unproven business plans and limited track records. If a commercial space is attractive to numerous types of retail stores and service providers, an owner should have many options when seeking to lease or re-lease the property.

LEASE TERM

The shorter a lease, the sooner a tenant will have the ability to vacate a property or renegotiate a lower lease rate. This is especially true when demand for commercial space is limited and when rental rates are suppressed.

Shorter lease terms can also increase a property owner's negotiation position in periods when rents are rising rapidly and when tenant demand is strong. Tenants having successful business operations in a specific location are often reluctant to move as well.

But there is generally a greater amount of comfort associated with properties having strong tenants with long and well-structured leases. For example, if you own a retail shopping center with an established supermarket leasing 60% of the usable space as the anchor tenant, a long lease is very beneficial. Having such a tenant attracts consumers and provides customers for other businesses within the entire shopping center such as restaurants, bars, and retail stores. Knowing that the supermarket will remain for the next 10 years provides reassurance to other tenants and to lenders.

A well-structured lease should provide proper security to the landlord and have reasonable terms allocating specific responsibilities between the landlord and the tenant. In addition, to protect the property owner against the risks of inflation, leases should have escalation clauses that automatically result in higher rental payments over time. For example, a 20-year lease may start at 9% per year based upon the property purchase price. Every five years, the lease may increase by 10%. Assuming the property was purchased for $750,000, the lease scheduled in Table 15.2 would be applicable.

As the twentieth year approaches, the investor would discuss potential actions with the tenant such as vacating the premises or negotiating a new lease and lease rate. Often such leases grant the tenant one or more options to extend a maturing lease by a certain number of years. For example, this 20-year lease might provide two five-year lease extension options under the same terms. If the tenant chose to exercise both options, the lease on the property would be extended for an extra 10 years (30 years in total). Such a lease would probably require the same 10% increase in rent every five years. Therefore, under the extension options, the lease rate would increase to 13.18% for years 21 through 25 and to 14.50% from years 26 through 30.

Tenants are sometimes provided with the option to purchase a property at some point in time. It is rare that a specific purchase price will be agreed upon for a date in the distant future. If prices rise dramatically and a property is worth more than its purchase option price, then an owner can be forced to sell the property for substantially less than its value. If a property is worth less than its purchase option price, a tenant can choose not to buy the property or renegotiate a lower price. Putting fixed prices into future purchase options can be disadvantageous to property owners.

Providing a tenant with a right of first refusal to purchase a property is a more common feature. Under such an agreement, an owner is required to offer his property to the occupying tenant at the same price that a third party is willing to buy the property. For example, if you have a buyer willing to pay $1 million for your property, a right of first refusal would allow the tenant to buy the

Table 15.2
Sample Annual Lease Rates—20-Year Lease

Purchase Price		$750,000
	Lease Rate	**Annual Rent**
Year 1	9.00%	$67,500
Year 2	9.00%	$67,500
Year 3	9.00%	$67,500
Year 4	9.00%	$67,500
Year 5	9.00%	$67,500
Year 6	9.90%	$74,250
Year 7	9.90%	$74,250
Year 8	9.90%	$74,250
Year 9	9.90%	$74,250
Year 10	9.90%	$74,250
Year 11	10.89%	$81,675
Year 12	10.89%	$81,675
Year 13	10.89%	$81,675
Year 14	10.89%	$81,675
Year 15	10.89%	$81,675
Year 16	11.98%	$89,843
Year 17	11.98%	$89,843
Year 18	11.98%	$89,843
Year 19	11.98%	$89,843
Year 20	11.98%	$89,843

property for $1 million. If the tenant chooses not to exercise its right, the property can be sold to the third party.

THE TRIPLE NET LEASE

The easiest type of commercial lease to manage from an owner's perspective is called a triple net lease. This means that the tenant is responsible for the payment of the three primary expenses associated with a property: maintenance, insurance, and taxes. Under a triple net lease, the tenant pays all costs associated with the property and the owner simply collects his monthly rent check.

I have seen many investors purchase individual, single-use properties under a triple net lease structure. These properties tend to have stand-alone buildings, such as a restaurant, gas station, bank, or retail store. Usually, investors will buy these properties from other investors or from the operator or franchisor of the business. For example, an investor may own a building that is currently being leased to a local bank branch. You might purchase the property from the investor and assume the lease. You become the property owner and landlord and the bank continues to pay you rent.

Using another example, assume a large drug store chain wants to sell some of the real estate it owns and uses to operate its drug stores. The company may prefer to lease certain locations rather than own them. There are many reasons for such decisions. A company might be trying to raise capital to open more stores or it may view renting a property as being a more efficient use of its time and investment dollars.

Under such circumstances, an investor could buy one or more properties from the corporation. As part of the agreement, the company might enter a 20-year, triple net lease and guarantee to make monthly rent payments for its term. Because triple net lease properties tend to be designed for very specific uses and are often required to conform to the specific franchising requirements of a particular store brand, the leases tend to be long. Assuming that reasonable escalation clauses are included in the lease, longer leases provide greater security to property owners.

Even though tenants are required to pay for the taxes, insurance, and maintenance costs associated with a property under a triple net lease, property owners must ensure that these expenses are being promptly paid. Tenants should be required to list owners as beneficiaries under property insurance policies. Tenants can also be required to provide evidence of payments to property owners of insurance and taxes. Properties can be visited and inspected from time to time to ensure proper maintenance as per the terms of each lease.

Often brokers represent buyers and sellers when seeking to purchase or sell commercial properties. Many brokerage firms list available triple net lease properties for sale on their Web sites. A large seller of such properties is Marcus & Millichap (marcusmillichap.com). Just remember that prices and many terms should be considered negotiable and an adequate estimated profit should be expected. I have seen many properties, particularly in strong upward climbing markets, sell for such high prices that the low projected returns made little sense for investors.

The triple net lease is widely accepted within the commercial real estate industry for retail-type properties. Other forms of lease require the owner to pay for virtually all property expenses, while some require the landlord and tenant to share the costs of specific items. The more tenants and the more complicated the lease structures, the more investors should rely on the expertise of an experienced real estate attorney. Regardless of the type of commercial property, an attorney should review the terms of any purchase and selling agreements and leases.

USE YOUR NETWORK

Because commercial real estate investing requires a level of expertise that is often unfamiliar to residential property owners, commercial real estate investors should learn from and rely upon industry professionals as much as possible. The greater risk associated with commercial real estate investing can lead to greater financial devastation if investors are not proactive and assertive.

A real estate attorney may be your greatest asset when seeking to acquire, own, and sell commercial properties. I suggest that investors entering the waters of commercial real estate investing use an experienced real estate attorney for all facets of a transaction, including the negotiation and review of purchase and sales documents, leases, financing agreements, and any other applicable documentation.

A property management firm that focuses on commercial real estate can be an invaluable resource when selecting properties, finding the best tenants, setting terms, and negotiating leases. Such companies can also take responsibility for monitoring tenant insurance and tax payment obligations when needed. Property management firms can target specific marketing efforts toward proper audiences of potential tenants as well.

While Realtors are often biased in their opinions due to the commissions they receive, they can provide a wealth of information when seeking to buy and sell properties. Ask about development and business trends in the general area, the type of tenants that would find a specific site desirable, the market level and stability of rents, etc.

Property inspectors and other consultants play a critical role when seeking to acquire a commercial property. Your goal is to know exactly what you are buying and to be able to reasonably anticipate any future costs and problems. What is the current state of the property? Are there any hidden repairs that are needed? What is the condition of the roof, parking lot, air and heating system, plumbing, etc.? How strong is the tenant and how reasonable and secure are any existing lease terms? Is the property prone to flood? Will flood or earthquake insurance be needed? What is the current and expected zoning for the property and the surrounding areas? These are some of the questions that experienced professionals can help you answer.

REAL ESTATE DEVELOPMENT

This book is not advocating that investors oversee their own real estate development projects. Rather, such specialized ventures should be managed by professional real estate developers that have successful track records, vendor relationships, and experience in construction and project oversight.

Investors can invest in such projects more passively. There are many real estate developers that continually seek investor capital to help finance a particular project. For smaller projects, usually land is acquired and individual houses or commercial buildings are constructed. Larger projects can include the development of entire residential communities or commercial sites such as office parks and hotels.

The profit potential when developing real estate is usually recognized when construction is complete and the finished properties are sold. This may occur fairly quickly or over long periods of time depending on the type of project and market conditions at the time of the expected sales. Some properties are leased and held longer term. Investors need to understand the expected time periods in which their dollars will be invested.

Investing in real estate development can be very risky. Taking a piece of land and preparing it for construction can be a significant process in itself. There are political hurdles, including different zoning and municipal codes that will dictate what you can and cannot build in a certain location on a certain piece of property. There may be environmental problems that must be resolved. All or a portion of a property could be in a flood zone. These are all items that must be addressed in advance before buying or building on a piece of land. Not only do you have to convince yourself, you also have to convince city officials and your lender that your development project makes sense.

Once you have your building permits and financing in place, the construction process presents a number of additional challenges and risks. Managing various tradesmen, adhering to design, and staying on a cost and timing budget require significant skill and sometimes luck. Many real estate developers are very successful and make huge profits. Others are less successful, projects fail and investors lose money. If you choose to invest with a particular developer, make sure that you are fully aware of his track record with prior projects and that he has proper experience and a favorable reputation.

The complexity and extent of the intended structure is a key variable in regards to the length of time a construction project can take. Other factors can also cause timing delays such as weather and the availability of tradesmen and other service providers. Whether you are using your money, a bank's money, or a combination, the longer a project takes to construct, the more the financing costs and the less available profit.

Once a building is complete, sometimes there remains the risk of finding a tenant or buyer. Such "speculative" development projects (those that start construction first and then focus on finding a tenant or buyer during construction or after completion) are substantially riskier than those having a buyer or tenant in place before starting construction.

Construction costs are another risk associated with development projects. Steel, glass, concrete, lumber, labor, and other required resources can have huge price escalations in fairly short periods of time. Many construction projects can take a couple years or more from start to finish, which leaves a significant period of time for costs to rise. I have seen many developers forced to stop construction because they could no longer afford a project. Banks were no longer willing to provide financing and the projects went into default. When this happens, the chances of equity investors getting their money back become slim.

Build-to-suit properties are development projects pre-leased before construction to tenants that require custom-built properties. The risk of finding a tenant is therefore eliminated in such projects. However, other risks become more apparent. Since build-to-suit properties are customized for a specific user, you are relying heavily on the strength and viability of a particular tenant. If the tenant does not renew its lease or if the tenant goes out of business, you may struggle to find another occupant.

When a customized property becomes vacant, you can first try to find another tenant that operates within the same franchise (i.e., another restaurant operator within the same chain). Your second choice might be another operator within the same industry (i.e., a restaurant operator within a different chain). In this case, you may be forced to pay for structural modifications to meet the new tenant's requirements or you may have to allow rent concessions if the tenant bears such expense. Alternatively, you might need to find a tenant in an entirely different industry (i.e., a shoe store operator taking the place of a restaurant operator). The costs and rent concessions in these circumstances can be quite large.

When investing in build-to-suit projects, careful attention should be given to the creditworthiness of the tenant and the initial lease term should be long enough and the rental rate high enough to pay for the building plus an appropriate profit.

PROFITABILITY

As with any real estate investment, a sufficient profit margin should be expected under reasonable circumstances. Investments having more risk should pay greater returns to investors. Longer term investments with poor liquidity should also provide higher profits when compared to similar shorter term opportunities.

When investing in passive investments, the expected profitability will vary with the risk associated with each investment. For example, you might expect the common stock of a publicly traded REIT to generate average annual returns of 8–12% in most years. When investing in a real estate development project with an expected term of three years, you might expect a 20–30% annual return due to the greater risks and limited liquidity involved.

There are always individual properties that need to be sold quickly or that offer a substantial value through some form of property improvement. Due to the lack of liquidity and the private nature of sales negotiations and transactions, real estate can be underpriced for a variety of reasons and provide great buying opportunities. But there will be times when investing in real estate generally does not make sense and finding good buying opportunities becomes more difficult. In such cases, investors may choose to be sellers rather than buyers.

Estimating a property's profitability often depends upon your investment strategy. If you plan to buy and hold a property long term, you should consider the profitability of the investment over some period of time.

When considering buy and sell investment strategies, profitability estimates should be more simplistic and include the costs to purchase, carry and make any needed improvements. Selling prices, costs, and holding periods should be conservative to provide room for any unexpected events.

It is important that investors properly assess the profitability of an investment before its acquisition. If you or one of your partners is unable to do so, you should probably consider a less complicated investment. Too many investors, both residential and commercial, have purchased properties without any type of rational investment approach. Randomly buying a property and assuming that it will immediately and continually rise in price is an unreasonable expectation.

SUMMARY

Commercial real estate investing has varying levels of risk. While there are many additional complexities associated with commercial properties when compared to residential properties, there are also significant profits to be made when investing in the commercial markets. In addition, being able to invest in both residential and commercial real estate can provide investors with additional diversification benefits and expand the number of investment opportunities.

It takes many years to develop the expertise needed to own and manage large commercial properties. For those investors having the desire to enter the commercial real estate markets, I suggest adhering to a slow and methodical approach. When seeking direct property ownership, individual investors should consider simpler properties and lease structures with lower risk. Also, ensuring adequate cash flow to weather expected and unexpected cycles and events is critical to maintaining holding power.

Industry professionals are essential resources when considering the purchase or sale of commercial property. In particular, an experienced real estate attorney can save you significant sums and prevent you from making irreversible mistakes. Knowing exactly what you are preparing to buy or sell arms you with the knowledge of a prudent real estate investor and can lower your risk exposure dramatically.

Chapter 16

COMMERCIAL REAL ESTATE INVESTING: CASE STUDIES

CASE STUDY I

Investor:	Jeff Greene
Occupation:	City roadway maintenance worker
Real estate experience:	Buyer and seller of residential properties over the past 12 years; currently owns five residential properties in Nashville, Tennessee
Property management:	Self-managed
Primary investment strategy:	Buy-and-hold
Current market conditions:	Up commercial market with normal appreciation expected to continue

Overview

Jeff has a strong understanding of the responsibilities associated with residential property ownership and management. He has negotiated the purchases and leasing of five single-family homes, a duplex, and a triplex during the past 12 years. In addition, Jeff chose to sell two single-family homes during this period to help purchase the duplex and triplex. When making the decision to sell, Jeff forecasted the profitability of owning the multiunit properties versus holding the two existing single-family homes. The upside of purchasing the larger properties was compelling enough to convince Jeff to sell the two existing properties.

Jeff has spent years building and strengthening a broad network of service providers, including Realtors, inspectors, lenders, and repair and maintenance people. In addition, Jeff has solid relationships with a local real estate attorney and his tax advisor.

Jeff feels confident in the knowledge and skills that he has acquired through residential real estate investing. He now wants to expand and further diversify his real estate portfolio by adding one or more commercial properties. Jeff recognizes the additional complexities associated with commercial real estate investing and decides to enter the market in a slow and methodical fashion. He plans to leverage his existing relationships with industry professionals and engage new service providers that specialize in commercial properties as needed.

Jeff is targeting small commercial properties under existing triple net lease structures with strong tenants. If the majority of an acquired property's expense and oversight can be the responsibility of the tenant, Jeff believes that he can forgo the services of a property management firm and manage the property himself. Doing so should significantly enhance the profitability of the investment.

Market Assessment

Jeff lives in a suburb outside of downtown Nashville. His rental properties are all located around the city. The duplex and triplex are located on the outskirts of the downtown area, while the three single-family homes reside in suburban neighborhoods further away.

The residential housing market in Nashville has been steadily increasing and fairly consistent during the past decade. Demographics, employment diversity and strength, and overall housing demand remain favorable. Jeff and various local housing experts are expecting normal appreciation rates in this market for the foreseeable future.

The commercial markets in and around Nashville are also perceived as being stable. Demand for commercial space is expected to continue to be supported by a major university, a diversified employer base, and favorable population increases.

The Team

The Realtor that Jeff has employed for several residential transactions has referred him to a colleague within the commercial realty division of her firm. Jeff has been impressed by the level of service and industry expertise shown to date. His commercial Realtor has provided excellent insights regarding the desirability of specific properties and locations. She is also able to provide sales, listings, and capitalization rate trends for available and recently sold properties.

Jeff's real estate attorney specializes in both residential and commercial real estate transactions. Jeff will use his services when negotiating purchase agreements and when evaluating any leases and other applicable documentation. As his properties and transactions have become larger and more complicated, Jeff has relied more and more on his attorney's services.

When Jeff sold each of his properties, his tax advisor assisted him with the facilitation of Section 1031 exchanges. By doing so, Jeff avoided substantial tax payments that would have resulted from the large gains that were embedded in these properties. Each time Jeff sold a property, shortly afterward he identified and ultimately purchased an additional property. This allowed him to transfer his tax basis from a sold property to a purchased property and avoid and defer the payment of any capital gains taxes.

Jeff has a strong relationship with two local banks and a mortgage broker. He has proven to be a successful, diligent, and knowledgeable real estate investor. Jeff has borrowed, repaid, and refinanced numerous loans on his various residential properties. In addition, he has made a logical progression by gradually increasing the number and types of properties that he owns and manages.

Jeff has discussed his interest in purchasing a small commercial property with his lenders. They feel that Jeff is employing a relatively low risk and reasonable approach based upon his investment strategy and the types of properties he is targeting. Jeff has been given initial feedback regarding potential financing terms. As specific properties are identified, his lenders will provide more specific proposals.

Jeff has established relationships with inspection firms capable of assessing the condition of any commercial properties considered for purchase. Jeff wants to ensure that existing tenants are properly maintaining properties under their lease terms and that any hidden problems are discovered.

Target Market

Since Jeff plans to oversee the commercial property management functions, he is considering properties in the Nashville vicinity within reasonable driving distance. He targets properties in areas that are expected to have stable and potentially increasing demand.

Jeff is willing to purchase a commercial property costing between $500,000 and $650,000. He believes that his local bank will lend him approximately 75% of the purchase price. While this is a large investment for Jeff, the relatively low purchase price will limit his buying opportunities to a small number of properties within the commercial real estate market.

Jeff is targeting properties having existing leases with strong tenants. Since this will be his first commercial investment, Jeff wants to minimize his risk exposure by targeting properties in attractive locations having one or more tenants with significant periods of proven operating success. Jeff also focuses on the financial strength of the tenants guaranteeing the leases and upon leases that have substantial remaining terms.

Property Selection/Valuation/Projected Profitability

Based on Jeff's investment parameters, his Realtor made appointments to visit several properties during the past few weeks. These investment opportunities included a small bank branch, two restaurants, a combined convenience store and gas station, and a property leased to a retail tenant.

After visiting each property, Jeff prepared a table (16.1) to compare some of the key characteristics of each property and lease.

The offering prices for the properties ranged from $550,000 to $725,000. Property 1 is in a great location with an extremely strong tenant. However, this property would most likely be outside of Jeff's price range. In addition, because the property presents such low risk, it also appears to provide the least profitability under its current lease. Jeff also considers the specificity of the property's use and the costs involved if the property ever needed to be leased to a tenant within

Table 16.1
Commercial Property Comparisons

	Property 1	Property 2	Property 3	Property 4	Property 5
Offering price	$725,000	$650,000	$575,000	$550,000	$625,000
Net operating income (NOI)	$54,375	$67,425	$47,000	$54,725	$50,000
NOI capitalization rate	7.50%	10.37%	8.17%	9.95%	8.00%
Location	Excellent	Moderate	Good	Fair	Good
Tenant	Local bank	Gourmet restaurant	Fast food restaurant	Convenience store and gas station	Sporting goods store
Tenant history	5 years	1.5 years	12 years	4 years	8 years
Tenant strength	Strong	Questionable	Strong	Moderate	Strong
Remaining lease term	5 years	3.5 years	8 years	3 years	12 years
Rent escalation clause	1.5% per year	Annually inflation indexed	10% every five years	2% per year	Annually inflation indexed

a different industry. Also, the fixed annual rent escalation clause within the bank's lease of only 1.5% would subject Jeff to potential inflation risk each year. Jeff realizes that the average annual inflation rate is over 3%. An increase in rent of only 1.5% per year would result in lower purchasing power and lower expected annual appreciation.

The NOI capitalization rates of the visited properties ranged from 7.50% to 10.37%. The higher cap rates tended to be for shorter leases and for leases with tenants having weaker credit strength. For example, Property 4's NOI is $54,725 and its offering price is $550,000 (a NOI cap rate of 9.95%). A higher NOI cap rate implies greater profitability for a buyer (at least initially). However, Property 4's convenience store and gas station tenant has only three years remaining on its lease and the general area where the property is located has been deteriorating. In addition, the financial statements provided by the selling broker indicate material tenant sales declines for the past three years.

Jeff perceives the chances of the tenant vacating Property 4 at the end of its lease as being probable. At such time, lower demand for the property could result in substantial vacancy time, a lower lease rate, and a resulting lower property value. In addition, since the property has been used to store and sell petroleum products, it is probable that environmental problems will exist. Converting the property to anything other than a gas station may result in huge expenses.

Jeff realizes that he will most likely need to settle for lower profitability in return for lower risk. Properties having higher NOI cap rates tend to have greater risks than properties having lower NOI cap rates. This is generally because lower risk properties provide lower returns to investors.

The quality of a property's location will often determine its long-term value regardless of its current use and lease terms. Jeff excludes Property 2 from his list, in part, based upon its mediocre location. In addition, the tenants operating the restaurant are a husband and wife team with limited financial strength and a relatively short history of operation. In addition, Jeff believes that gourmet restaurants and other luxury service providers will be adversely affected during economic downturns.

After performing his initial research, Jeff has narrowed his selection process down to Property 3 and Property 5. Both are in good locations and have strong tenants with successful operating histories and long-term leases. While dependent upon negotiations and further diligence, Jeff's first choice is Property 5. He feels that the longer lease term and the rent escalation clause within the lease with the sporting goods store is more attractive when compared to Property 3. In addition, Jeff feels that Property 5 is more generic and will appeal to a greater breadth of tenants if re-leasing is ever necessary.

Negotiation Process

Jeff realizes that sellers having weaker properties and tenants are most likely to provide the greatest price concessions. While Jeff's decision to bid on the stronger and more desirable properties may cost him more and result in lower perceived initial profitability, Jeff believes that such properties will encompass less risk and provide greater profitability over the long term.

Jeff's Realtor advises him that the sellers of Property 3 and Property 5 are both individuals. Neither seller is interested in providing any type of seller financing and they are both receiving current rent and are in no hurry to sell. In addition, both properties have been on the market for less than 45 days and each property has been receiving substantial interest. Jeff's Realtor has been told by the Realtors of each seller that one or more offers on each property have been received and rejected to date.

The commercial real estate markets have been very stable in Nashville and the outlook remains favorable. While current market conditions are generally more advantageous toward sellers than buyers, Jeff believes that the local commercial real estate market is fairly valued and that substantial upside potential exists. Jeff decides to make an offer on Property 5.

Jeff's initial offering price was $590,000, which was about a 5.5% discount to the seller's asking price. His offer contained terms such as extended closing and contingency timelines, relatively large repair allowances and that the seller pay the buyer's closing costs. The seller countered at a price of $620,000, which was less than a 1% discount to the asking price. In addition, the seller materially altered most of the terms of Jeff's initial offer to make them more favorable to the seller.

The discussions went back and forth for a couple days before a final price of $610,000 was agreed upon. This was a discount of approximately 2.5% when compared to the initial asking price. During the discussions, Jeff and his Realtor attempted to use non-price related terms as negotiating tools to drive the pricing down as low as possible. Ultimately, a short financing and inspection contingency period, a large deposit, and a promise to close the transaction within 30 days were important commitments to the seller. Jeff was pleased with the final purchase price and terms.

Financing

Jeff continued to receive feedback from two lenders as he worked through the property selection process. He learned that both lenders favored properties leased to retail tenants far more than properties leased to restaurant and convenience store and gas station operators. Additionally, financing a property leased to a gourmet restaurant provided them with the least amount of comfort. Like Jeff, both lenders believed that such a business had the least chance of surviving any type of material economic downturn or recession. Such feedback was helpful to Jeff when deciding which properties to pursue.

Because the properties Jeff was targeting were so small, Jeff found that local banks were the most viable source of financing. Neither bank would lend against a property without a personal guarantee by Jeff. Before accepting, Jeff needed to know that he could make the debt and maintenance payments associated with his purchased property if it were to become vacant. After assuming unfavorable scenarios within his entire real estate portfolio, including the vacancy of the commercial property and one or more of his residential properties for an extended period of time, Jeff felt comfortable that he would have adequate cash flow to meet his payment obligations under adverse circumstances. He therefore agreed to provide a personal guarantee.

Jeff was able to avoid any type of financial covenants associated with the property and his personal financial condition. There were clauses that allowed the bank to reappraise the property if needed and require full repayment of the loan if a material reduction in value occurred. Jeff's attorney advised him that this was standard language for a lender that was rarely ever enforced.

Before deciding which lender to use, Jeff negotiated the best terms he could from each bank. He then modeled the different options to determine which was the most profitable. In addition, he qualitatively assessed the payment structure of each option to ensure that he was not exposing himself to too much risk.

Jeff agreed to a 75% loan-to-value ratio with a fixed interest rate of 7%. Since the final purchase price of the property was $610,000, Jeff's lender agreed to provide approximately $457,500 of this amount at the time of purchase. Jeff also agreed to a seven-year loan with a 20-year amortization schedule. The longer amortization schedule will lower the amount of principal repaid each month and also lower his monthly payment. However, the remaining principal balance of the loan will be due at the end of seven years. Jeff will need to either sell the property or refinance the loan before its maturity date. As part of his modeling, Jeff created the loan amortization schedule in Table 16.2.

Table 16.2
Loan Amortization Schedule

	Beginning Balance	Monthly Payment	Interest	Principal	Ending Balance
Month 1	$ 457,500	$ 3,547	$ 2,669	$ 878	$ 456,622
Month 2	456,622	3,547	2,664	883	455,738
Month 3	455,738	3,547	2,658	889	454,850
Month 4	454,850	3,547	2,653	894	453,956
Month 5	453,956	3,547	2,648	899	453,057
Month 6	453,057	3,547	2,643	904	452,153
Month 7	452,153	3,547	2,638	909	451,244
Month 8	451,244	3,547	2,632	915	450,329
Month 9	450,329	3,547	2,627	920	449,409
Month 10	449,409	3,547	2,622	925	448,483
Month 11	448,483	3,547	2,616	931	447,553
Month 12	447,553	3,547	2,611	936	446,616
Month 13	446,616	3,547	2,605	942	445,675
Month 14	445,675	3,547	2,600	947	444,727
Month 15	444,727	3,547	2,594	953	443,775
Month 16	443,775	3,547	2,589	958	442,816
Month 17	442,816	3,547	2,583	964	441,852
Month 18	441,852	3,547	2,577	970	440,883
Month 19	440,883	3,547	2,572	975	439,908
Month 20	439,908	3,547	2,566	981	438,927
Month 21	438,927	3,547	2,560	987	437,940
Month 22	437,940	3,547	2,555	992	436,948
Month 23	436,948	3,547	2,549	998	435,950
Month 24	435,950	3,547	2,543	1,004	434,946
Month 25	434,946	3,547	2,537	1,010	433,936

	Beginning Balance	Monthly Payment	Interest	Principal	Ending Balance
Month 26	433,936	3,547	2,531	1,016	432,920
Month 27	432,920	3,547	2,525	1,022	431,899
Month 28	431,899	3,547	2,519	1,028	430,871
Month 29	430,871	3,547	2,513	1,034	429,838
Month 30	429,838	3,547	2,507	1,040	428,798
Month 31	428,798	3,547	2,501	1,046	427,752
Month 32	427,752	3,547	2,495	1,052	426,700
Month 33	426,700	3,547	2,489	1,058	425,643
Month 34	425,643	3,547	2,483	1,064	424,578
Month 35	424,578	3,547	2,477	1,070	423,508
Month 36	423,508	3,547	2,470	1,077	422,432
Month 37	422,432	3,547	2,464	1,083	421,349
Month 38	421,349	3,547	2,458	1,089	420,260
Month 39	420,260	3,547	2,452	1,095	419,164
Month 40	419,164	3,547	2,445	1,102	418,062
Month 41	418,062	3,547	2,439	1,108	416,954
Month 42	416,954	3,547	2,432	1,115	415,839
Month 43	415,839	3,547	2,426	1,121	414,718
Month 44	414,718	3,547	2,419	1,128	413,590
Month 45	413,590	3,547	2,413	1,134	412,456
Month 46	412,456	3,547	2,406	1,141	411,315
Month 47	411,315	3,547	2,399	1,148	410,167
Month 48	410,167	3,547	2,393	1,154	409,013
Month 49	409,013	3,547	2,386	1,161	407,852
Month 50	407,852	3,547	2,379	1,168	406,684
Month 51	406,684	3,547	2,372	1,175	405,509
Month 52	405,509	3,547	2,365	1,182	404,328
Month 53	404,328	3,547	2,359	1,188	403,139
Month 54	403,139	3,547	2,352	1,195	401,944
Month 55	401,944	3,547	2,345	1,202	400,742
Month 56	400,742	3,547	2,338	1,209	399,532
Month 57	399,532	3,547	2,331	1,216	398,316
Month 58	398,316	3,547	2,324	1,223	397,092
Month 59	397,092	3,547	2,316	1,231	395,862
Month 60	395,862	3,547	2,309	1,238	394,624
Month 61	394,624	3,547	2,302	1,245	393,379
Month 62	393,379	3,547	2,295	1,252	392,127
Month 63	392,127	3,547	2,287	1,260	390,867
Month 64	390,867	3,547	2,280	1,267	389,600
Month 65	389,600	3,547	2,273	1,274	388,326
Month 66	388,326	3,547	2,265	1,282	387,044
Month 67	387,044	3,547	2,258	1,289	385,755
Month 68	385,755	3,547	2,250	1,297	384,458
Month 69	384,458	3,547	2,243	1,304	383,154
Month 70	383,154	3,547	2,235	1,312	381,842
Month 71	381,842	3,547	2,227	1,320	380,522
Month 72	380,522	3,547	2,220	1,327	379,195

Table 16.3
Five-Year Property Cash Flow

	Year 1	Year 2	Year 3	Year 4	Year 5
Rental payments	$ 50,000	$ 51,500	$ 53,045	$ 54,636	$ 56,275
Debt payments	(42,564)	(42,564)	(42,564)	(42,564)	(42,564)
Property cash flow	$ 7,436	$ 8,936	$ 10,481	$ 12,072	$ 13,711

Jeff estimates the return on his investment by looking at the net cash flow expected to be generated from the property and by using a discounted cash flow analysis. Since the lease on the property is triple net and since Jeff is not paying a third-party property management firm, there are no expected expenses other than his loan payments. Table 16.3 forecasts the net cash flow associated with the property during the first five years.

As can be seen in Table 16.3, the net cash flow from the property will continue to rise as rents increase by the annual rate of inflation (assumed to be 3% per year) while loan payments remain constant.

In Table 16.4, Jeff assumes that the property is sold after five years using an 8.2% NOI cap rate, which is the same cap rate used when purchasing the property for $610,000 ($50,000/$610,000 = 8.2%). The gross sales price of $706,874 is derived by taking the expected rent in Year 6 of $57,963 (Year 5's rent increased by 3%) divided by 8.2%. The real estate commissions and property closing costs are assumed to be a percentage of the gross sales price. At the time of sale, the loan to the bank must be repaid. The balance owed to the bank after five years can be found in Jeff's amortization schedule in Table 16.2.

As indicated in Table 16.4, Jeff forecasts his cash equity in the property at the end of five years as being approximately $273,372. Jeff's initial down payment when purchasing the property was approximately $160,000. This consisted of the 25% of the purchase price that was not financed by his lender ($610,000 times 25% = $152,500) plus attorney fees, a .50% origination fee to the bank (0.50% times $457,500 = $2,288), and some minor additional closing costs.

Table 16.5 uses the assumptions derived in Tables 16.3 and 16.4 to perform a discounted cash flow analysis. Jeff starts by including his initial cash outflow of $160,000 in the first period. He then uses the annual property cash flows

Table 16.4
Sale of Property after Five Years

Sales price after five years (NOI cap rate of 8.2%)	$	706,874
Real estate commissions (5%)		(35,344)
Closing costs (0.5%)		(3,534)
Debt repayment (balance at the end of Month 60)		(394,624)
Remaining equity	$	273,372

Table 16.5
Discounted Cash Flow Analysis

	Time of Purchase	Year 1	Year 2	Year 3	Year 4	Year 5
Initial cash outflow	$ (160,000)	$ —	$ —	$ —	$ —	$ —
Property cash flows (Table 16.3)		7,436	8,936	10,481	12,072	13,712
Sales proceeds (Table 16.4)						273,372
Net cash flows	$ (160,000)	$ 7,436	$ 8,936	$ 10,481	$ 12,072	$ 287,084
Average annual investor return						16.49%

provided in Table 16.3 for Years 1 through 5. Jeff also includes the amount of cash he expects to receive from the sale of the property in Year 5 ($273,372 from Table 16.4) after paying closing costs and repaying the bank.

The analysis in Table 16.5 was performed in Microsoft Excel. By including every source and use of cash from the time Jeff purchases the property to the time Jeff sells the property, the results show an estimated average annual return of 16.49% per year. This means that if Jeff's assumptions are accurate, he will earn an average annual return of 16.49% for each year that he holds the property. Jeff is pleased with the profit potential of his new investment.

Property Management

Since the tenant is responsible for the costs associated with maintaining the property and for property tax and insurance payments, Jeff does not feel the need to hire a property management firm. In addition, Jeff's attorney has thoroughly reviewed the lease with the sporting goods store and believes that it is very secure and that it adequately protects Jeff's rights as owner.

Jeff will continue to physically inspect the property from time to time to ensure that it is being properly maintained. Jeff can drive by the property and walk the parameter and interior as needed. In addition and if needed, the lease allows Jeff to have the property more thoroughly inspected after providing reasonable notice to the tenant.

The tenant's insurance provider will be notified that Jeff will be the new property owner. Jeff will be listed as the beneficiary under the policy and he will assign this right to his lender. The insurer will be instructed to mail duplicative statements to Jeff. In addition, the tenant is obligated to provide Jeff with proof of payment for each insured period. These requirements give Jeff comfort that he can properly monitor the payment of insurance and that he will receive advance notification if payment under the policy ever becomes delinquent. If such an event were to occur, Jeff would have time to make the payments under the policy to ensure that coverage does not lapse.

The tenant is also responsible for providing evidence to Jeff that property taxes have been paid each year. Jeff can also periodically call or search the county records online to confirm that tax payments have been made.

The tenant has 12 years remaining on its lease. Under the triple net structure, the tenant is responsible for the costs associated with the property. Assuming the tenant performs as expected, Jeff's role as property manager will be very limited. Besides inspecting the property from time to time, Jeff's primary duties will entail collecting his monthly rental checks and paying his lender each month.

Conclusion

Jeff was prudent before purchasing his first commercial real estate property. He first acquired substantial knowledge through various types of residential real estate investments. Jeff slowly increased his portfolio and learned the responsibilities associated with single-family, duplex, and triplex property ownership. Jeff has bought and sold properties. He has negotiated with sellers and buyers and has worked with different lenders to finance and refinance properties. Jeff has built a solid network of industry professionals and service providers.

When seeking his first commercial investment, Jeff sought properties, tenants, and locations that would lower his risk exposure and provide him with significant upside potential. Jeff targeted favorable locations having good traffic, visibility, and site access. In addition, he focused on triple net leases that transfer the primary responsibilities of property ownership to the tenants. By having a tenant with a proven history of successful operations, financial strength, and a lengthy lease term, Jeff has conservatively entered the commercial real estate market and has chosen an investment that is well positioned for future appreciation.

CASE STUDY II

Investor:	Nancy Wynn
Occupation:	Commercial Realtor
Real estate experience:	Investor in limited liability company (LLC) owned by approximately a dozen individuals used for commercial property investing throughout Northern Nevada
Property management:	Third-party management firm
Primary investment strategy:	Property improvement
Current market conditions:	Down market characterized by trending sales declines and lower prices

Overview

Nancy has been a commercial real estate agent for almost 15 years. She is knowledgeable about the industry and well qualified to make commercial real estate investments. Nancy is particularly familiar with the Northern Nevada commercial real estate markets. This is the region where Nancy's Realtor activities take place and where she and her colleagues have personally invested.

Nancy has been investing with the same group of people for the past seven years. She was one of the founding members of a LLC formed to focus on commercial property acquisitions, improvements, and sales.

Nancy and her partners focus solely on commercial properties, primarily targeting retail and office buildings. The group believes that there is greater profit potential in commercial versus residential real estate investing. However, Nancy and her colleagues have always felt the need to maintain a diversified real estate portfolio. By pooling investor capital, the group has been able to purchase a greater number of properties and spread their risk among numerous investments. In addition, by combining investor capital, their investment entity has increased purchasing power and can acquire and own larger properties. Also, by partnering with other investors, each individual is able to benefit from the enhanced experience of the team. For example, some of the other members include two real estate developers, an attorney, and an accountant.

Market Assessment

The commercial real estate markets in Northern Nevada have been declining for the past few years. Nancy and her partners believe that many local markets are getting close to bottom. During their most recent monthly investment meeting, the following items were discussed:

- In many cases, commercial properties are being offered at sales prices that are near or below replacement cost.
- Capitalization rates have been rising steadily, but the rate of increase has slowed for the last several months.
- During the past few years, the general economy has been sluggish and businesses have been slow to spend money and expand operations. Economic data over the past year has been mixed and signs of favorable economic growth have become more frequent.
- Vacancy rates have trended higher during the past few years, but it appears that such numbers may be starting to stabilize.
- Tenants have been able to command more influence in negotiating attractive lease terms due to the greater availability of commercial space.

Property Selection

One of the real estate developers on the team has identified a property to be considered by the group. He has prepared the following summary to help facilitate initial discussions:

- The property is a 40,000-square-foot office building on approximately 1.5 acres of land located in Reno, Nevada.
- The property is approximately 10 years old and is in good physical condition.
- Several key tenants have vacated within the past few years due to the economic downturn. The vacancy rate of the property is approximately 40%. While the building has historically suffered from an above normal vacancy rate, greater focus and professional attention to the property should result in substantially higher occupancy levels through enhanced leasing and property management efforts.
- There are currently seven tenants, including a bank, an insurance company, a government agency, and several other reputable businesses. Most leases reflect current market rates and have initial terms ranging from three to five years. However, two of the leases representing approximately 8,000 square feet are significantly underpriced. Both leases expire during the next one to two years.
- The property is considered to be a Class B office building, meaning that its location, construction, and tenant quality are all good.
- The interior of the building shows very well. The exterior could use some improvement to better compete with other office buildings in the surrounding areas. Relatively small upgrades to the lobby and façade (the principal front of the building) would make a significant improvement and add substantial curb appeal.
- By enhancing the appearance of the exterior so that the building is more competitive with Class A structures and providing a greater focus on leasing and property management, this investment provides the potential to raise occupancy levels and rental rates substantially. In addition, lease rates can still be 15–20% less than competing office space in the same area.
- The expected cost of the property is approximately $125 per square foot (about $5 million). In addition, the costs required to renovate and improve the property are

estimated to be approximately $15 per square foot, resulting in total costs of about $140 per square foot or $5.6 million. This total cost is estimated to be around 40% below the cost required to purchase the underlying land and construct a new building.

- The ultimate goal of the investment would be to increase rental income and NOI by adding new tenants and renegotiating existing leases.
- Rumors are that the seller lacks holding power and is experiencing negative cash flow due to being overleveraged on the property.

Financing

The pooling of investor equity provides a strong capital base for the investment group. The individual investors would be unable to purchase the types of properties that the LLC is able to target. In addition, an entity having such financial strength that is owned by so many reputable industry professionals is perceived to be an attractive borrower by most lenders.

The partners speak to a few lenders regarding potential financing alternatives for the purchase of the property and for the needed improvements. A two- to three-year bridge loan seems to be a sensible option. Such a loan would "bridge" the project from the time of purchase through the period of renovation and the point of sale. A typical bridge loan would have an initial two-year term but would also provide for a one-year extension at the borrower's option.

Local bankers seem willing to lend up to 75% of the property's value. An origination fee of 1% of the loan amount would be due at the time the property was purchased and the loan was provided. In addition, a 0.5% extension fee would be payable to the lender after two years if the borrower decided to extend the loan for an additional year.

The bridge loan would require interest-only payments on a monthly basis at a fixed rate of 7.5%, then the repayment of the total principal amount at the end of either 24 or 36 months depending upon whether or not the extension option was exercised. If the project cannot be sold within the three-year period or the partners decide to hold the property longer term, the bridge loan could be refinanced with more appropriate financing depending upon the circumstances and desires of the partners at such time.

As the LLC owned by Nancy and her partners has grown in size and become more diversified, the entity has been able to borrow from various lenders on a non-recourse basis. This means that personal guarantees are not necessary. Each loan is secured by a specific property but also by the partner's equity within the entity.

Valuation/Projected Profitability

The bank loan is assumed to cover 75% of both the purchase price and the property-improvement costs (75% times $5.6 million results in a $4.2 million loan). Based on the expected purchase price, property-improvement costs, and financing terms, Table 16.6 estimates the cash investment required by the partners to be approximately $1.5 million.

This is a large investment for Nancy and her partners. Before making such a commitment, they want to be assured that they will earn a reasonable return on

Table 16.6
Project Investment

Purchase price	$	5,000,000
Closing costs		50,000
Loan origination fee		42,000
Property improvements		600,000
Total cash needed	$	5,692,000
Bank financing		(4,200,000)
Investor equity investment	$	1,492,000

their investment, particularly since the local commercial real estate market may continue to decline.

The success of the project is based upon significantly increasing NOI over a two- to three-year period. In addition, the selling NOI cap rate is also critical. As markets decline, cap rates rise to reflect the higher profitability demanded by investors and/or the expected declines in NOI and property values.

Any rise in cap rates from the time that Nancy and her partners purchase the property to the time of its sale can offset some or all of the benefits derived from any increases in NOI. For example, if a property generates $350,000 in NOI and is purchased for $5 million, the resulting cap rate is 7% ($350,000 divided by $5 million equates to a 7% cap rate). If the NOI of such an investment is increased to $400,000, one would expect the property to rise in value. However, if at the time of sale cap rates for similar properties have risen to 8%, there will be no increase in value ($400,000 divided by an 8% cap rate still equals a value of $5 million).

Table 16.7 shows how the team plans to increase NOI by improving the property and by finding additional tenants and raising a portion of the existing rents through more aggressive leasing and property management. Debt payments, leasing costs, and tenant improvement allowances are not part of the computation of NOI but will be considered in the calculation of net cash flow.

As can be seen in Table 16.7, the tenants are responsible for repaying the property owner for shared expenses such as utilities, security, and telephone, which results in additional property revenue. Property management expense is increased each year to reflect the greater costs associated with additional tenants and increased management efforts. Capital reserves are amounts put aside each period to cover future expenditures.

After forecasting NOI, the team wants to ensure that there is enough cash flow being generated from the property to cover the interest payments that would be required under the loan. In addition, in order to achieve the level of NOI being targeted, substantial leasing efforts and tenant improvement allowances will be incurred. Leasing agents will be paid commissions each time a new tenant is found for the property. Costs in the form of tenant improvement allowances will also be incurred to customize the space being offered to each tenant prior to occupancy.

Table 16.8 accounts for the additional expected cash outflows associated with debt payments, leasing commissions, and tenant improvements. The payments

Table 16.7
Current and Forecasted Net Operating Income

	Time of Purchase	Year 1	Year 2	Year 3
Property revenue				
Rental income	$ 592,500	$ 651,750	$ 782,100	$ 844,668
Expense reimbursement	26,663	22,811	27,374	29,563
Total revenue	619,163	674,561	809,474	874,231
Property expense				
Property management	17,027	25,296	30,355	32,784
Property taxes	62,500	70,000	72,100	74,263
Insurance	5,850	6,000	6,180	6,365
Utilities	92,874	101,184	121,421	131,135
Accounting and legal	888	2,500	2,575	2,652
Repairs and maintenance	67,500	72,500	77,000	79,000
Security	2,182	2,247	2,315	2,384
Telephone	2,083	2,145	2,210	2,276
Capital reserves	4,200	4,326	4,456	4,589
Total expense	255,104	286,198	318,612	335,448
Net operating income	$ 364,059	$ 388,363	$ 490,862	$ 538,783

on the bank loan are assumed to be interest-only at 7.5% for each year. An additional loan extension fee is assumed to be paid in Year 3 so that the loan can be extended for an additional year. The cash flow from the project is expected to increase significantly as the property's occupancy rate is raised.

If Nancy and her colleagues are successful, they will improve the NOI dramatically over the next few years. But they need to make sure that they can still make money assuming a continued decline in commercial real estate values and rising cap rates. They hope that they are purchasing the property near the bottom of the current real estate cycle, but such a determination is highly subjective and impossible to gauge for certain.

Table 16.9 shows how much the property might be worth depending on the NOI shown in Table 16.7 for each year and by assuming varying selling cap rates.

Table 16.8
Property Cash Flow

	Year 1	Year 2	Year 3
Net operating income (Table 16.7)	$ 388,363	$ 490,862	$ 538,783
Debt payments	(315,000)	(315,000)	(315,000)
Loan extension fee			(21,000)
Leasing commissions	(18,555)	(19,112)	(19,685)
Tenant improvement allowance	(64,553)	(66,490)	(68,484)
Property cash flow	$ (9,745)	$ 90,260	$ 114,614

Table 16.9
Estimated Selling Prices

NOI Cap Rate	Current Value	Year 1	Year 2	Year 3
6.50%	$5,600,895	$5,974,801	$7,551,718	$8,288,960
6.75%	$5,393,454	$5,753,512	$7,272,025	$7,981,962
7.00%	$5,200,831	$5,548,030	$7,012,310	$7,696,892
7.28%	$5,000,000	$5,333,792	$6,741,529	$7,399,675
7.50%	$4,854,109	$5,178,161	$6,544,823	$7,183,765
7.75%	$4,697,525	$5,011,123	$6,333,699	$6,952,031
8.00%	$4,550,727	$4,854,526	$6,135,771	$6,734,780
8.25%	$4,412,826	$4,707,419	$5,949,839	$6,530,696
8.50%	$4,283,037	$4,568,965	$5,774,844	$6,338,617

If the property is purchased for $5 million, based upon the property's current NOI of $364,059 shown in Table 16.7, the resulting cap rate is approximately 7.28% ($364,059 divided by $5 million equals 7.28%).

The investment group focuses primarily on the values shown in Year 3. They believe that it will take two to three years to maximize the property's value and the team does not want to sell the property too soon and forgo substantial profit potential.

If the local commercial real estate market improves within the next three years, the property could be sold at a lower cap rate than the 7.28% used to value the property at the time of purchase. However, the commercial real estate markets in Northern Nevada peaked several years ago and have continued to decline ever since. If this downturn worsens, there is the possibility that a higher cap rate will be required to value the property at the time of sale.

The best case scenario shown in Table 16.9 assumes a sale based on Year 3 NOI and the lowest cap rate of 6.50%. By taking the Year 3 NOI in Table 16.7 of $538,783 and dividing this number by a cap rate of 6.50%, the property's value would be estimated to be $8,288,960. The worst case scenario shown in Table 16.9 reflects a selling cap rate in Year 3 of 8.50%. In this case, the selling price would only be $6,338,617.

Table 16.10 was prepared to better understand the project's attractiveness when using the most profitable cap rate of 6.50% and the least profitable cap rate of 8.50% reflected in Table 16.9. As can be seen in Table 16.10, the sales proceeds vary dramatically depending upon which cap rate is assumed.

Table 16.10
Estimated Sales Proceeds

	6.50% Cap Rate		8.50% Cap Rate	
Sales price	$	8,288,960	$	6,338,617
Debt repayment		(4,200,000)		(4,200,000)
Realtor commissions		(497,338)		(380,317)
Closing costs		(82,890)		(63,386)
Investor sales proceeds	$	3,508,732	$	1,694,914

Table 16.11
Discounted Cash Flow Analysis with 6.50% Cap Rate

	Time of Purchase	Year 1	Year 2	Year 3
Investor equity investment (Table 16.6)	$ (1,492,000)			
Property cash flow (Table 16.8)		(9,745)	90,260	114,614
Investor sales proceeds (Table 16.10)				3,508,732
Net cash flow	$ (1,492,000)	$ (9,745)	$ 90,260 $	3,623,346
Annual investor return	35.70%			

The partners realize the other primary risk besides the selling cap rate. If the NOI of the property cannot be increased as expected, then the value of the property at the time of sale will be lower than the values derived in Tables 16.9 and 16.10. However, the team believes that increasing the property's NOI is achievable based upon the planned improvements and the tenant incentives that will be offered.

The final analyses shown in Tables 16.11 and 16.12 were prepared by Nancy and her colleagues to consolidate the work prepared within the prior tables and to forecast the total profitability of the investment under two alternative outcomes.

Table 16.11 performs a discounted cash flow analysis to assess the expected annual profit earned from the investment assuming the higher sales price resulting from a 6.50% cap rate. At the time of purchase, the investor group invests $1,492,000 as indicated in Table 16.6. The net cash flows expected to be generated by the property for Years 1 through 3 are taken from Table 16.8. In addition, the investor sales proceeds expected to be realized in Year 3 under the 6.50% cap rate scenario are taken from Table 16.10 and are also included.

Table 16.12
Discounted Cash Flow Analysis with 8.50% Cap Rate

	Time of Purchase	Year 1	Year 2	Year 3
Investor equity investment (Table 16.6)	$ (1,492,000)			
Property cash flow (Table 16.8)		(9,745)	90,260	114,614
Investor sales proceeds (Table 16.10)				1,694,914
Net cash flow	$ (1,492,000)	$ (9,745)	$ 90,260	$ 1,809,528
Annual investor return	8.31%			

If the assumptions in Table 16.11 materialize over the next few years, Nancy and her partners will earn an average annual return of 35.70% on their investment. However, this outcome assumes the property achieves its targeted NOI and that it can be sold based upon a 6.50% cap rate.

Table 16.12 is identical to Table 16.11 except that an 8.50% selling cap rate is assumed. This table was created to show a less favorable outcome assuming that the commercial real estate market continues to decline and cap rates continue to rise. While an 8.31% annual return is not as favorable as the team would like, this scenario provides substantial room for additional deterioration in the local market and still provides an acceptable outcome.

Nancy and her partners completed this analysis to better understand the investment opportunity and to help quantify a possible range of upside and downside possibilities. Having a logical investment strategy greatly increases the probability of success and now the team is better prepared to focus on the variables that are critical to the profitability of the project.

Other Considerations

Nancy and her colleagues will determine the best course of action for the property over time. If the Reno commercial real estate market is unfavorable during the next few years, the team can decide to hold the property for a longer period than initially forecasted. The group feels confident that the property can be refinanced at the end of three years if needed. The fact that the property is generating a substantial amount of cash flow is an attractive feature to lenders.

The team is willing and able to exercise holding power if needed. The cash flow from the group's other investments can be used to support the project if needed. Alternatively, if the market rapidly improves and the property performs well or if an attractive offer is received, the group may decide to sell earlier than originally expected.

Summary

Nancy and her partners are experienced commercial real estate investors. Their primary investment strategy revolves around finding undervalued retail and office properties that can be improved to generate greater value over fairly short periods of time. Usually this entails finding properties that have been mismanaged and that have deferred maintenance. The unique individual areas of expertise allow each group member to benefit from the enhanced experience of the team. To date, Nancy and her colleagues have been successful in increasing the value of properties by improving appearances, raising occupancy levels, and adjusting below-market rents. This strategy allows the team to find opportunities and make money in all real estate markets.

CASE STUDY III

Investor:	Frank Hill
Occupation:	Landscaper in Phoenix, Arizona
Real estate experience:	Limited to passive mutual fund investments
Property management:	N/A
Primary investment strategy:	Passive with ability to hold investments long term
Current market conditions:	Flat with market turnaround expected over the next few years

Overview

Frank has no direct real estate investment experience besides the ownership of his own home. He does not want the responsibility of owning investment property. However, Frank believes in maintaining a diversified portfolio of investments. In addition, he understands that real estate can enhance his total portfolio performance and reduce the volatility of his annual returns.

Frank's investment portfolio consists of various stock and bond mutual funds held within his employer's 401K plan, and an Individual Retirement Account (IRA) and general brokerage account with a reputable investment firm.

The mutual funds that Frank has chosen invest primarily in domestic and foreign stocks and bonds. Additionally, approximately 10% of his investments are held within a mutual fund that invests in REITs. This fund owns the common stock of over 100 REITs that invest in a variety of real estate sectors both domestically and abroad. This allows Frank to obtain diversified exposure to hotels, apartments, warehouses and self-storage facilities, retail shopping centers, and many other types of properties.

Frank is now considering an investment being offered by a local real estate developer. The project includes the purchase of land and the construction of a small retail shopping center. Once construction is complete, the property is planned to provide rental space for three retail tenants. Once the property is fully leased, it is expected to be sold for a profit. Frank wants to be diligent before considering the investment. In addition, he does not want it to represent more than 5% of his total portfolio.

Market Assessment

Commercial real estate markets have had varying performance across the country, but generally values and rents have been fairly stagnant for the past few years. These market conditions were preceded by rapid and unjustified appreciation in many residential housing markets across the country which helped lead to a national economic downturn several years earlier. Following general pricing declines in residential and commercial real estate, land and commercial properties have experienced flat pricing with little activity for several years. Many analysts believe that the overall economy and the corresponding demand for commercial property by businesses will improve in the near to mid-future.

Frank realizes that local markets behave uniquely. When assessing a specific investment opportunity, he needs to consider the specific location and current and expected market trends. He knows that traffic count, site accessibility, and surrounding businesses and activities are all important factors.

The specific investment opportunity is located within an upper-middle class neighborhood just outside the city of Phoenix. During a rapidly rising residential housing market, many new homes and subdivisions were created in the surrounding areas. While there are still a fair amount of homes that need to be sold, the community has established a strong population base.

A supermarket opened on an adjacent lot to the targeted property 18 months ago and appears to be doing well. The developer is expecting to lease the completed property to reputable tenants. A national coffee shop and a well-known movie rental company are expected to be two of the tenants. The third tenant could be a dry cleaner or small restaurant or dentist or other professional. Frank agrees with the developer that such businesses would be well received in the specific community.

Investment Assessment

The developer held a formal presentation for investors. Based on this presentation, some documents that were also provided, and his own perceptions, Frank determined the following:

- The developer has an impressive background and significant expertise in managing construction projects. He is well known within the Phoenix area and has a successful track record making money for his investors. The developer's partner is a property management and leasing specialist and has relationships with numerous potential tenants. She is responsible for negotiating and structuring tenant leases and has worked with the developer on several prior projects.
- The developer has been focused on the specific property for several years. Now that land prices have fallen, he believes that the project provides an opportunity for abnormally high profits. In addition, construction costs have also declined due to the lower demand for such services under slowed market conditions.
- At the time the property is acquired, a three-year lease will be signed with the coffee shop and a five-year lease will be signed with the movie rental store. Both leases will be guaranteed by corporations having substantial financial strength. Having the property mostly pre-leased prior to construction significantly reduces the risk of the project.
- The developer will receive a monthly fee equal to an annual rate of approximately 1.5% of the expected gross revenues from the fully leased property for overseeing the construction, leasing, and sales processes. This appears to be a reasonable fee for such services.
- The equity provided by Frank and other investors will be used to pay for the land. A local bank will provide a construction loan to cover the costs of completing the project and to provide time to sell the property. None of the investors will be required to personally guarantee the loan. If the property cannot be sold prior to the maturity date of the loan, the developer and his partner feel confident that the loan can be refinanced based upon the strong tenants and the contractual scheduled rent payments.
- The property will be acquired and held by a newly formed LLC. Frank and other passive investors will be Class I owners of the entity. The developer and his partner will be Class II owners.

- When the property is sold, after repaying bank debt, other expenses, and the investor's original investment, any profits will be allocated first to the Class I investors until they receive a 20% annual return. Any profits remaining will be split 50/50 between the Class I and Class II investors. This profit-sharing structure motivates the developer and his partner to maximize the project's performance since they will not be allocated any profits until after the investors receive a 20% annual return.
- The developer's financial modeling shows estimated total profits to the Class I investors of over 28% per year. These numbers are based on a total investment period of two years and a NOI selling cap rate of 8.5%, which assumes no improvement in current market conditions. Other higher selling cap rate scenarios provided by the developer result in annual profits to investors of at least 12%. Such scenarios were provided to show downside possibilities if market conditions deteriorate prior to the time of sale.

Conclusion

Frank believes that he has thoroughly researched the investment opportunity. He feels confident in the developer and his partner's ability to successfully manage the project and achieve the targeted objectives. The fact that the property will be substantially pre-leased prior to starting construction reduces its risk dramatically and makes it much easier to finance and ultimately sell.

Frank likes the profit potential of the investment. However, he does not want to become swayed by greed and invest too much of his net worth into one investment. Frank understands and values the benefits of diversification and plans to limit his total real estate exposure to no more than 15% of his total investment portfolio. Frank also evaluates his liquidity needs over the coming years and feels comfortable that he can commit the capital without concern that he will unexpectedly need the funds.

.

INSTRUCTIONS FOR REAL ESTATE ACQUISITIONS MODEL

WARNING!

This Real Estate Acquisitions Model is a sample tool provided to assist investors when evaluating the estimated profitability of a potential real estate acquisition. The model was designed primarily to assess single-family residential homes being purchased as rental properties. The projected profitability provided by the model is only hypothetical and in no way guarantees any future results. The results of the model are highly dependent upon the assumptions assumed by the user. This model should not be used as the sole determinant when deciding whether or not to purchase a specific property. Rather, it should be used as one of many tools and perspectives when evaluating the qualitative and quantitative aspects of a particular property and its assumptions and results should always be reviewed for reasonableness. The model is based, in part, on the use of traditional financing sources with loan-to-value (LTV) ratios of less than 100%. Assuming more aggressive and less generic forms of financing could provide misleading results.

ASSUMPTIONS

Remember that the model assumes an investment holding period of five years. This does not mean that you will hold the property for five years. You may sell it sooner or later. The five-year hold is a somewhat random period used to capture any assumed appreciation. Any estimated appreciation and any monthly income or loss factors into the Average Annual Expected Return calculation.

You must have a sufficient version of Microsoft Excel (Excel version 2003 or higher) to open and use the model. To access and download the model, visit my Web site at www.LawlessInvesting.com. There is a "macro" in the model that is required to perform the calculations. If asked by your computer, in order for the model to work properly, you must allow the macro to be enabled. In addition, some computers may disable the macro due to the security level on the computer being too high. In order for the model to work properly, you may need to lower the security level on your computer before downloading the file. Your security level can be reset to the higher level after you have downloaded the model.

Once the file is open, you will see various assumptions needed to perform the analysis and ultimately produce the Average Annual Expected Return. These assumptions are numbered from 1 through 20. The numbers that are required to be inputted by the user of the model are shown in red. The user can only change the numbers in red and is responsible for the accuracy of each of these figures. If a specific income or cost category is not appropriate, either enter zero or leave it blank for each relevant period. Any number highlighted in red will factor into the model's results (the computation of the Average Annual Expected Return).

The numbers provided in the initial model are only intended to provide an example and these figures should be changed or deleted to reflect the user's personal circumstances.

A description and some helpful hints regarding each assumption are listed below.

1. *Rental Income*—Enter the amount of monthly rent that you expect to receive from one or more tenants over a five-year (60-month) period. You should have a good idea of what typical market rents are for similar pieces of property in similar locations. Make sure to account for any limitations that your property might have that could lead to lower rents and longer vacancy times. In addition, make sure that you consider the time needed to prepare a property for rent and to find initial and future tenants. Also consider any vacancy time when trying to sell the property.

2. *Average Annual Appreciation Rate*—This is your expectation of how much your property will appreciate in value each year based on annual compounding. For example, if you purchase a property for $200,000 and you expect it to increase in value by 5% per year, the model will assume a value of $210,000 at the end of the first year ($200,000 times 1.05), $220,500 at the end of the second year ($210,000 times 1.05), etc. Depending on the time period covered, long-term home prices have historically appreciated between 3% and 5% per year across the United States. Please recognize that these are only averages and that different areas of the country have substantially higher and lower appreciation rates at different points during each corresponding real estate cycle. As you can imagine, this assumption has a significant effect on the Average Annual Expected Return produced. It is up to you to assume a reasonable appreciation rate before purchasing a property.

3. *Repair Costs to Prepare Property for Sale*—Normally, when you sell a property, the buyer will have a professional inspection performed to determine its condition. These inspections are very thorough and include reviewing foundations, air conditioning and heating units, electrical systems, and tiling and general plumbing. You can expect that, in most cases, the buyer is going to ask you to either repair some or all of these items or request some type of discount from the sales price to cover these costs. The model is based on assuming a percentage of the gross selling price to estimate these costs. For example, assuming .50% for repair costs at the time of sale and a $200,000 selling price will result in costs of $1,000 ($200,000 times .50%). If needed repairs were deferred during your ownership, this number could be substantially larger.

4. *Realtor Commissions at Time of Sale*—Realtors can be critical when selling a property. The more challenging current real estate market conditions, the more value a Realtor can add. As seller, you are paying your Realtor and the buyer's Realtor a commission for arranging the sale. The buyer does not normally pay either. Depending on how well you negotiate, typical Realtor commissions are generally between 4% and 7% of the gross sales price.

5. *Non-Realtor Closing Costs at Time of Sale*—There are always additional closing costs required to sell a property and they can vary significantly by state. Such fees can include state taxes and title agent cost and they can sometimes be shared differently between buyer and seller depending on the property and location. I usually assume an average cost of .50% to 1.00% of the gross sales price, but this number can vary fairly significantly by state and transaction, so you should research the expected costs.

6. *Purchase Price*—This is the gross price that you will pay to acquire the property. I often find that the model, along with other research, helps me to back into a maximum price that I am willing to pay a seller.

7. *Mortgage Loan-to-Value*—Your lender will base your loan amount on some LTV ratio. A LTV ratio of 80% is typical for residential housing, but some lenders are willing to go higher. In such cases, the interest rates are usually higher as well, but the model should help you to determine which type of financing is most attractive.

8. *Annual Interest Rate*—The model assumes a fixed rate of interest for the five-year holding period. Enter the annual interest rate that you expect to receive from your lender. If you intend to use a floating rate loan to finance your purchase, you will need to assume a fixed rate of interest for the model (i.e., an estimated average interest rate over the five-year holding period). Floating rate loans add additional uncertainty when forecasting, so they can add more risk to your profitability estimates.

9. *Monthly Mortgage Term*—This is to compute principal amortization on your loan. You want to enter the number of months that the loan's amortization schedule is based upon. Often times, a loan's maturity date and its amortization period are the same. For example, a 30-year loan might be due in 30 years and also amortize over 30 years. In this case, you would enter 360 months (30 years times 12 months per year). However, some loans have different maturity dates and amortization schedules. For example, a loan may be due in five years and amortize over 15 years. In this case, you would use 15 years and enter 180 months (15 years times 12 months per year). The model assumes the same loan is outstanding for the full five-year holding period.

10. *Loan and Property Closing Costs*—There are usually costs associated with purchasing a property that a lender will charge such as appraisal and document fees. In addition, in order to receive a lower interest rate, many lenders will charge some type of origination fee. Title companies or lawyers will also assess costs for the services that they perform, including title searches to ensure that the property has no existing liens and document preparation fees. Also, there may be specific state taxes due as a result of transferring the property. To simplify the model, all such "closing costs" need to be aggregated into one number and entered into this line of the model. It is up to you to properly assess these expected fees by obtaining quotes and estimates from your lender and title company or attorney.

11. *Up-front Costs Required to Prepare for Occupancy*—Before renting a property, there are often repairs that must be made to make the property suitable for occupancy. Such costs can include carpet cleaning or replacement, painting, tiling, and electrical and plumbing repairs. The magnitude of these costs can have a significant

effect on the profitability of a property and must be carefully considered. A home inspection is a great first step. Once any current and potential problems have been identified, you can request quotes and estimates from various vendors to better quantify these expected costs and assess the condition of the property.

12. *Average Monthly Insurance*—The model assumes an average monthly cost for insurance covering the property. Make sure that this number is entered as an average monthly number for Years 1 through 5. If you receive an annual quote from an insurance agent, be sure to divide the annual premium by 12 before entering it into the model.

13. *Average Monthly Real Estate Taxes*—The model assumes an average monthly cost for real estate taxes on the property even though such taxes are often due less frequently depending on the property location. However, many times lenders will pay these taxes on your behalf and require that monthly payments for real estate taxes be added to your monthly mortgage payment. Again, make sure that you enter an expected average monthly number for each year. Also, when obtaining property tax estimates, remember that some states provide tax concessions for primary home-owners. As soon as a property is purchased for investment purposes, the property taxes could rise. In addition, your purchase price could trigger a higher property valuation for tax purposes and also result in higher taxes going forward.

14. *Average Monthly Homeowners' Association Dues*—Some properties require peri-odic payments to a homeowners' association to cover costs associated with common areas within a residential community. This may include landscaping services and/or the costs of maintaining certain resident amenities (i.e., pools, fitness facilities, etc.). Such fees should be disclosed by the seller of the property. Beware of homeowners' associations that are poorly funded and that have historically required special (and unexpected) assessment fees from property owners. These fees should also be entered into the model as an expected average monthly cost for each year.

15. *Average Monthly Repair Costs*—It is virtually impossible to know exactly how much a particular property will require in owner repair costs. However, these expenses are important when forecasting expected profitability and must be included in the model. Depending upon variables such as the age of your property, the type of tenants, and weather conditions, your property may have more or less ongoing expenses. In many months, you may have little (if any) repair costs. How-ever, when something major needs replacement or repair (i.e., a roof or heating and air conditioning system, painting, plumbing, etc.), you may be looking at large dollars. For forecasting purposes, you must estimate the average monthly repair costs for each of the five years.

16–20. *Other Monthly Expenses*—Since each property is unique and may have more or less specific costs and expenses when compared to other properties, assumptions 16 through 20 allow the model user to define and input any additional average monthly costs and expenses that are not covered in the prior categories. For these items, you can change the description to properly describe the specific expenses associated with your property and input the expected average monthly costs for each year. Like all the assumptions in the model, if a certain cost or income category is not applicable to your specific property, just leave the item blank or zero and the model will ignore this category.

Average Annual Expected Return—After entering all of your income and expense assumptions, you are now ready to compute the Average Annual Expected Return for a specific property. A formula is embedded within the model that calculates this number once you click on the ''Compute'' button at the top, left-hand side of the page.

The Average Annual Expected Return is the estimated amount of profit you will earn each year over the assumed five-year holding period. For example, if you enter all of your income and expense assumptions for a particular property and the Average Annual Expected Return is computed to be 10%, this means that by purchasing and holding this asset for five years, you are projected to earn approximately 10% per year for each of the five years (assuming your assumptions are accurate).

As mentioned above, be careful with this investment tool. The output of any model is only as good as the inputs being assumed by the user. Use this model as one of many methods to assess a property's fair value and profitability potential. If the model tells you that you can pay $200,000 for a property and earn an Average Annual Expected Return of 12% when the property is being offered for sale at $150,000, then something is definitely wrong. Never pay more than market pricing for a property and always double check and recheck your assumptions.

INDEX

About the Author

Robert E. Lawless has held several executive level positions, including senior vice president, chief financial officer, and treasurer, at several private and publicly traded companies owning and managing billions of dollars of real estate investments. Lawless is a Certified Public Accountant, a Chartered Financial Analyst, and a Certified Treasury Professional. He holds the Series 7, Series 24, Series 27, and Series 63 securities licenses. He also has an MBA from Vanderbilt University and is the author of *Retire Richer and Faster! You Can Manage Your Own Financial Independence!*